The Memoir of John Durang

Playbill for Durang's performance in York during his Pennsylvania Dutch summer tour

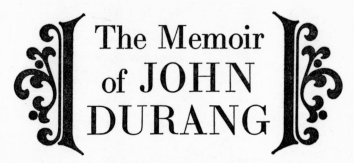

The Memoir
of JOHN
DURANG

American Actor
1785–1816

Edited by Alan S. Downer

Published for
The Historical Society of York County
and for the American Society for Theatre Research
by the University of Pittsburgh Press

Library of Congress Catalog Number 66–10729

Copyright © 1966, The Historical Society of York County

Manufactured in the United States of America

Preface

JOHN DURANG'S MEMOIR of his experiences on the American stage during the early days of the nineteenth century is one of the cherished artifacts in the archives of The Historical Society of York County. It was obtained in 1945 from a local dealer with funds raised by Mr. James W. Shettel, an officer of the Society and a student of the American stage. Other than knowing that the Memoir was in possession of Charles Durang, son of John Durang, in 1866, and that it subsequently turned up in the hands of a Philadelphia dealer in 1940, The Historical Society has no record of its early history or whereabouts.

Since its acquisition the Society has been seeking ways to make the Durang story available to the public. On May 17, 1963, the American Society for Theatre Research was approached and through the efforts of Alan S. Downer of Princeton University (editor of the Society's publication, *Theatre Survey*) an agreement was reached with the University of Pittsburgh Press to publish the book with Mr. Downer as editor.

The Historical Society of York County is pleased to be

associated with the American Society for Theatre Research and the University of Pittsburgh Press in this undertaking.

ROBERT P. TURNER, *President*
The Historical Society of York County

In preparing the manuscript for the press, I acknowledge with gratitude the contributions of John M. Clum, research assistant, Leyton Horner, former director of The Historical Society of York County, Howard Rice of the Princeton University Library, and Hubert Heffner, of the University of Indiana, who generously shared the results of his own research into the early history of the American stage. The inclusion of the illustrations was made possible by a grant from the Princeton University Research Fund.

A. S. D.

Contents

PREFACE   v

ILLUSTRATIONS   ix

INTRODUCTION   xi

DURANG'S MEMOIR

Part One: ["The Greatest Dancer in America"]   3

Part Two: Durang's Tour to Canada   47

Part Three: [With the Chestnut Street Theatre]   95

Part Four: A Memorandum and Abstract Journal Taken from
My Day Book   127

NOTES   143

APPENDIX TO THE NOTES   155

REFERENCES   165

INDEX   167

Illustrations

Frontispiece

Playbill for Durang's performance in York

during his Pennsylvania Dutch summer tour

Following page 76*

Durang in character of the Dwarf metamorphosed

Road to St. John. Cross on the left hand

Cap Saunta Chapple. Road to Quebec

Durang in character of a Hornpipe

Durang in character of the Dutch Fisherman

Durang in character of a Highland Fling

Durang in character of Harlequin

Durang in character of a Pas seul à Vestris

End papers

"Poney Race with Real Ponies at the Pantheon and

Ricketts's Amphitheatre, Philadelphia, Jan'y 14th 1797" †

* John Durang's watercolors are owned by The Historical Society of York
County. They are reproduced through the courtesy of the Society.

† The endpapers are reproduced from a sepia found in Durang's memoir.
The signature reads "J. Galland, Ser."

Textual Devices

[. . .]   A word or words missing and not conjecturable.

[ ]   A number or part of a number missing or illegible.

[roman]   Conjectural reading for missing or illegible matter. Missing letters and minor words, such as articles, which were not questionable have been inserted without brackets.

[*italic*] Editorial comment inserted in the text (except on pages 122–124, where the playwrights' names have been set in roman type).

⟨*italic*⟩ Matter deleted in Durang's diary but restored in this text.

and   Used for "&" except in the form "&c."

For other alterations of the original text, see page xvii of the Introduction.

Introduction

THE FIRST CENTURIES of American history are a history of pioneers: pioneers in forest and field, in politics, industry, science, and occasionally in literature and the arts. Since the theater is privileged or condemned to be a mirror of the experience of its audiences, the early history of the American stage is equally a history of pioneers. William Dunlap begins his story of the Hallams, our first firmly established professional troupe, with a somewhat fanciful account of organizing a federation on the ship that brought them from England, recalling no doubt the Pilgrims organizing their confederation on the *Mayflower*. And as the first emigrants were forced to live off the land, so these early actors furnished their tables with game shot from the windows of their dressing rooms. No dwelling places awaited the settlers of Virginia or Massachusetts, so they built their own; no theaters awaited the first actors, so they built their own. Finding the natives suspicious or hostile, the early pioneers huddled together for defense or won over the opposition by compromise or chicanery or immobilized it with firearms, fireworks, or firewater. The actors never engaged their opponents, the puritanical theocrats of the Atlantic shores, in open warfare, but the stratagems and tricks to which they resorted for survival are not without their political analogues: they bribed the authorities by offering performances for the benefit of the indigent or circumvented them by disguising their plays as concerts or moral lectures.

Propagandists were quick to make political virtue out of the pioneers' necessity: the strength of the republic derived from the muscle and the axe, unenfeebled by reliance upon inherited institutions, family traditions, conventional education. American artists, when they began to appear, were celebrated in similar terms (overlooking, for example, Franklin's admission that his prose style was based on a close study of Addison and Steele, or the years of English apprenticeship served by such painters as Peale and West). It was the proudest of the many boasts of Edwin Forrest and his followers that he was a self-taught actor, and he would often buoy up a sinking box office by advertising himself "in American letters," that is, in line capitals farced with stars and stripes.

It may seem strange that, in this nation-wide addiction to chest-thumping and image-building, no one seized on the career of John Durang, who was born in Lancaster, Pennsylvania, eight years before the revolution and died in Philadelphia seven years after the end of the War of 1812; was a member of Hallam's company when it reopened the theater in New York in 1785; became a prominent member of the first American circus troupe; and was certainly the first to play Shakespearean leads in Pennsylvania Dutch. Although his only formal training was as apprentice to a dancing master, he painted scenery, built playhouses, performed acrobatic and equestrian feats, constructed a puppet show, developed summer amusement parks, organized and directed acting companies, founded a short-lived theatrical dynasty, devised transparencies, pyrotechnic displays, and pantomimes, and played minor roles in legitimate drama.

It was the minor roles that kept him out of the histories of the theater and the memoirs of national apologists. Durang was always on the fringes of theatrical respectability: he was generally to be seen in the entr'actes and afterpieces of the legitimate or in the circus ring or in the taverns and stage stops that served as playhouses between Philadelphia and Harrisburg. His success, if it had been noticed, would have been an embarrassment to the propagandists: America's self-esteem demanded comparison at the top. Dunlap equates the Hallams, who were in actuality a bankrupt, third-rate London company, with their contemporary David Garrick; and William Wood, whose company Durang served for twenty years, does not mention him in his *Personal Recollections of the Stage.*

Fortunately, Durang himself does not seem to have been aware of his delinquency. Sometime after 1816 he composed a memoir of his theatrical career. He obviously intended it for publication, for pasted into the holograph are a set of his own watercolors of himself in various characters and of scenes observed on his travels, with keys in the text indicating where they are to be inserted. Whether because it was never completed or because of Durang's lowly status in the theatrical hierarchy, the memoir went unpublished—but not unused. It was mined by Durang's son, Charles, for his history of the Philadelphia stage (1854) and by Elizabeth Clarke Kieffer for the only extended biographical account of Durang in *The Dutchman,* vol. xxi, 1954. One excerpt has been printed as Durang wrote it: "The Circus First Comes to Albany, 1797" in *New York History,* January 1963. It is the barest justice that after more than a century and a half his wishes should be realized.

Something more than justice to Durang is involved in the publication of his account of his life. Records of the beginnings of the theater in America are not so ample and detailed that any document can be lightly dismissed. While Durang is reticent about domestic matters he is remarkably full in dealing with his profession. And, however crude his own painting, he had an artist's eye for the significant detail, the characteristic gesture. His memory may play him tricks when it comes to chronology, but it rarely fails in recapturing the essence of a story.

From his account, also, emerges a vigorous self-portrait. He recalls the delights of the village life of his childhood, the excitement as the local militia prepared to join in the War for Independence. He remembers Philadelphia, newly freed of British occupation, and Dr. Franklin sitting by as the boy was fitted into costume for a patriotic festival. We see him captured by the enchantment of the stage, fearful of parental disapproval, yet manfully determined to follow his adolescent yearnings. Show business possesses him wholly: he will learn to dance, to leap over horses, to tumble, to walk the slack wire, whatever his profession seems to be demanding. He will undertake the ordinary perils of stagecoach and packet travel and learn through experience—though a shrewd man with a shilling—that extra expenditures diminish risks. But he is also willing to strike out into what was still a wilderness to practice his profession in an unknown land. "I was not fond," he says, "of an inactive life."

In nearly forty years of industrious application to a variety of theatrical efforts, nothing is more characteristic than the summers between 1808 and 1816 when he organized "fit-up" companies to develop the Pennsylvania Dutch circuit. A fit-up in itself was nothing new; summers were slack times for metropolitan theaters in England as well as America. To bridge the gap between spring closing and autumn reopening, minor players would often form themselves into groups to tour summer resorts or communities too small to support regular theaters. The nucleus of Durang's fit-up, as was traditional, was his own family with three or four other minor players to round it out. Their offerings were more music hall than legitimate: entertainments of singing, dancing, acrobatics, with an occasional farce or recitation to fill up the bill. But Durang, by cutting the text or doubling roles, would frequently offer a legitimate play, *The Stranger*, perhaps, or *She Stoops to Conquer*. Knowing his audience, he included an occasional piece in German, an afterpiece like *Stoffle Rilbps* or *The Seu-Shwain Wedding*, or Shakespeare's *Richard III*.

The quality of such performances must remain unjudged. Certainly Durang was attentive to business, expected his fellows to be, and devised schemes to keep them on their toes. The new governor of Pennsylvania, and leading citizens in other communities, who must have been able to make comparisons with the theaters of Philadelphia and Baltimore, were his willing supporters. Innkeepers and landlords with halls to rent were cooperative year after year and gladly stored his theatrical gear over the winter in prospect of his return. At the very least, he does not seem to have disappointed the expectations of his audience, or feel obliged to apologize for professional shortcomings.

Indeed, unlike the most famous of all theatrical autobiographies, Durang's memoir is in no sense an apology for his life. The epigraph from *Othello* which he chose for his title page is neither defiance nor false humility, although it had become the customary cant of autobiographers. He emerges as independent and self-reliant, frugal and imaginative, industrious and alert to the opportunities of the moment. Like nature, he abhorred a vacuum and was eager to fill it with any one or several of a variety of professional skills that would leave a latter-day performer, in an age of specialization, aghast. He was a Jack-of-all-theatrical-trades and, at least in his own eyes, a master of a good many.

That he should be a literary man is too much to expect. His memoir lacks both the grace and the irony of a Colley Cibber or the anecdotal fluency of a Joseph Jefferson. But it is far from a flat record of events, and his personality triumphs over his syntax: the memoir speaks with his authentic voice. That as much of his voice as possible remain unmuffled, the text is here presented very much as Durang left it. Besides the textual devices described on page x, only minor corrections and alterations have been made. Capitalization and punctuation have been modernized for the convenience of the reader, and the abbreviation *whos.* is expanded to *whose;* but Durang's spelling remains essentially his own. It is not the spelling of an uneducated man; Durang had attended the German school of Christ Lutheran Church in York. There is a consistency in certain of his deviations from orthography (e.g., *where* —and at times *whare* and *whear*—for *were*), and these have been preserved, not just for the interest of linguistic scholars, but that his voice may speak to the modern reader.

In the fashion of his time, Durang says little about his family life. Of his wife, Mary McEwen, the marriage register notes only that she was white and a spinster. She may have appeared occasionally on the stage as a dancer, but her three sons and two daughters seem to have claimed most of her energies. She died of tuberculosis in Harrisburg, September 5, 1812, at the age of forty-four. His oldest son, Charles, was born December 4, 1794, and at the age of

eight made his debut as a dancer at the Chestnut Street
Theater in Philadelphia. Like his father, he was a man of
many talents: actor, ballet master, author, and stage manager. In 1854 he began serial publication in the Philadephia *Sunday Dispatch* of "The Philadelphia Stage from
the Year 1749 to the Year 1855, Partly Compiled from
the Papers of his Father, the late John Durang." This
valuable, if undisciplined, record was never printed in
book form. He died in 1870.

Ferdinand, Durang's second son, was born in Hartford in
1796. During the war of 1812 he enlisted with his older
brother and, while they seem to have had little opportunity
for battlefield heroics, they were chief figures in a historic
event in a tavern attached to the Holliday Street Theater in
Baltimore. The occasion is related by Chief Justice Tawney,
brother-in-law of Francis Scott Key:

Key read the words [of his poem] aloud, once, twice,
three times, until the persons present were electrified by
the pathetic eloquence. An idea seized Ferdinand Durang.
Hunting up a volume of old flute music, he impatiently
played snatches of tune after tune, as they caught his eye.
One called "Anacreon in Heaven" struck his fancy and
riveted his attention. Note after note fell from his puckered
lips, until with a leap and a shout, he exclaimed, "Boys,
I've hit it!" and fitting the tune to the words, there rang
out for the first time the song of the Star-Spangled Banner.
[York *Dispatch,* March 13, 1945.]

If John knew of his son's exploit, he is silent. But as one
who could rise to any patriotic occasion, he would have

approved. Ferdinand died of tuberculosis in 1831 while a member of the company at the Bowery Theater in New York.

Augustus, the third son, was born in Philadelphia in 1800 and made his debut as Tom Thumb at the Chestnut Street Theater. Here he was seen by the traveling star, Thomas Apthorpe Cooper, who took him to New York where he appeared at the Park, December 17, 1806. Later he gave up acting to become a sailor and was lost at sea.

Two girls completed the household. Charlotte was born in Philadelphia in 1803, danced in her father's summer companies, and died in 1824. Juliet, born two years after Charlotte, managed something more of a career. A dancer, she began in the family troupe, graduating to the Lafayette Theater in New York in 1825 and to the Bowery in the next year. In 1831 she made her debut as an actress at the Chestnut Street Theater in Philadelphia and, as Mrs. Godey, advanced to leading roles in provincial companies. She later married James Wallace, a minor actor who forsook the stage to become editor of the Philadelphia *Sun*. She died in Philadelphia in 1849.

Later generations of Durangs seem to have eschewed the stage, although Edwin Forrest Durang, Charles' son, was the architect of the Opera House in York, Pennsylvania.

John Durang's Memoir,

of His Life

and Travels.

To Which is Prefix'd a Short Tratise

of His Father's, Mr. Jacob Durang's,

Emigration to America.

..I Shall nothing Extenuate,
..nor set Down aught in Malice

PART ONE

["*The Greatest Dancer in America*"]

M R. JACOB DURANG, Senior, a native of Stras-
bourg, enter'd the French army when he was very
young in the Regiment de Waldner.[1] He continued in the
same regiment twelve years in the reign of Louis the 16th.
He being of a gay cheerful disposition, the colonell placed
him under his special favour. He was consign'd to the
surgeons of the army, where he made some proficiency in
the skill and knowledge of surgeory. He continued in that
occupation until he received the certificate of his discharge
to the esteem and honour to himself, and satisfaction to his
major and colonell. He had a prior promise in marriage
with Miss Joeann Catharine Arter, a native of Visenbourg
in the province of Alsace on the Rhine. He made his
arrangements conformably: the day after he obtained his
discharge, Feb'y 21st 1767, he married Miss Arter in
Visenbourg. They were both very young.

They both immediately set out on a journey for Holland,
where they took passage a cross the Atlantic for America.
They arrived safe in the harbour of Philadelphia, November 9th 1767. They proceeded on to Lancaster where Mrs.
Durang met with her sister married and settlet, which

enticed Mr. Durang and wife to settle for a time till circumstance should prevail, as the delicate situation of Mrs. Durang made it necessary; where thro' the divine favour of God, I was born in Lancaster, state of Pennsylvania, January 6th 1768.

America was at this time under the controlment of the British government, in the reign of George 3d. My father turn'd his mind on a permanent establishment. Little York in Pennsylvania proved a field to his advantage. The novelty of a man of his profession [2] so desired by the people of that place, with his customary address and politeness, accompany'd with the French and German language, soon gained the popularity of the inhabitance of Little York and its vicinity. By frugality and economy of my father and mother they soon gained the inheritance of respect and wealth. My father purchased a house and lot of ground in Market Street near the Courthouse (of late years it has been occupied for a tavern, sign of the Whitehorse) where they enjoy'd every desirable comforts of this life. My father had occasion twice a year to visit Philadelphia to purchase goods, as he keep a store in one part of the house, and such necesseries which could not be had in York, having it in his power, for he had provided everything necessary for a country life, horse and gig, cows, hogs, farming utensils, out lots, &c.

I was put to the German school, it being the most universal, as all the country in Pennsylvania was settlet by Germans. About this time as I was playing on a wheelbarrow, the barrow upset with me and broke one of my arms, which my father cured in a short time so well that I can't tell at this time which arm it was.

Yorktown is a dull place for business for merchants and most mechanics and inn keepers, except in seasons [3] when the fairs and harvest frolic are held. In those country towns the country people flock in from all quarters, old and young of both sexes; their native simplicity joined in sociability excite their mirth extensive. The market place is furnish'd with every description of fineries with some useful as well as ornamental goods by settle merchants [4] from Philad'a and Baltimore; all kinds of diversions going on during the whole day, the taverns crowded: in every room a fiddle, and dancing, bottles of wine on the table; showfolks with their signs out, hand organs and trumpits to invite the people to see poppet shows, wire dancing, slight of hand. They imposed their pretended conjuration so far on the harmless country people, with the threat to lock their mouth up with a padlock if they doubted their art. A great many marriages takes place by the young countrymen and girls at the time of their harvest frolics. Those frolics are an establish'd custom in Pennsylvania and will be held for many years to come. They encourage the young folks to work cheerful, to save as much money by their labour as will buy them useful and necessary things to please their fancy and enough left to pay their way in the frolic.

The Pennsylvania farmer stands predominant. He enjoys the sweets of industry and plenty in the bosom of his family. Their artless simplicity cements their harmony, and their barn is their best house. The greatest evil is a cohesion of gamblers who infest the country towns at the time of fairs, harvest frolics, and at the races. I have often look'd at them with what an egar devotion in their art they would draw the unsuspecting into their snare. And yet those very gamesters make the appearance of good morel citizens when they walk the streets of our capital cities.

In the Revolutionary War between North America and Great Britain, my father joined his brethren in arms [5] againsd tyrannic power in the glorious cause of liberty and religion, in defence and security of a home for their wives and children. My father was encamp'd at Lancaster. A regiment from Virginia lay in York. I prevail'd on my mother to make me a hunting shirt and trousers, green with yellow fringe. Thus equip'd I was constant with this Virginia encampment. The men where in a poor condition to meet an enemy: old and young, rich and poor, all in brotherly band, some with out shoes or stocking, some no coats, some with old muskets and some with fowling pieces, however as they went on their journey, whear supplied by citizens who could spare them clothes and provision. I set off with this regiment. When we arrived at the Lancaster encampment, my father soon sent me back to my mother in charge of a neighbour on horseback. I went home with a heavy heart.

During the winter General Howe and Kniphousen with

the British army lay in Philad'a. A number of British prisoners whare confined in the York and Lancaster jail. Several of the officers boarded at my father's house. They had an excelent band of music, and occasionally play'd at my father's to my great delight, and serenaded the citizens.

After the British evacuated Philad'a and New York, my father purchas'd property in Philad'a, a house in the center of the city. He sold his property in York and moved the family on to Philad'a. Soon after, the French army arrived. The fleet landed the troops (July 6th 1781) at Rhode Island; their march was conducted on thro' Philad'a in the greatest order. It was a grand sight. They made their encampment on the banks of Schuylkill, and in a very short time had bakers, tailors, blacksmiths, shoemakers, washing, cooking &c., all at work. The same regiment my father belong'd too, in France, was among those.[6] The colonell made his quarters at my father's house for a few days when they sat off on a march to join Gen'l Washington in the siege of Cornwallis.

Sometime before the French army arrived from France under Gen'l Rochambeau, in 1778, arrived the first ambassador from the Court of France to the United States, (his name) Sieur Gerard. His establishment was keep up in the most splendid stile, and did all in his power to amuse the citizens of Philad'a. He had all the ground where the new theatre and Shakespear buildings now stand for a pleasure ground, with a ball room in the centre of the lot, magnificently decorated, where he held his banquets and balls to the treat of the genteel citizens and strangers at large. The house he occupied for his domestic establishment stand on the ground to this day in Chestnut Street, off from the front of the street and opposide to his house. From the corner of Sixt and Chesnut whas then a vacant lot where occasionelly he gave splendid fireworks. His carriage was a heavy old fashioned mounted, the wheels like our Lancaster turnpike wagons, and low, the foot board behind large, with four footmen in red livery and gold lace, two coachmen on the large box seat in front, with a dog between them, in livery and cocked hats, 6 horses with eligant mounted trappings. His domestic household consisted of all men, not a woman in the house, but the head stuard, butler, head cook, with a bout 6 cooks under him and scullions, bakers, pastry cooks, valet de chambres, and porters. He seldom wrode in his carriage, but walk'd our streets like a plain American citizen. Numbers of poor families where supported from his house and table. The first pantomime I ever saw was performed by his household domestics in the old Theatre South Street.[7]

I cannot pass unnoticed a noted kind of lunatic character, one Jemmy de Rover, known by everybody as he followed the soliders from town to town, dress'd in regimetals and knapsack.

At this time the continental paper money was still in circulation and depreciateing. I heard my father say he gave one hundred and fifty dollars for a pound of butter, or tenpence silver.

The ice in Schuylkill braking up this winter showed [*shoved*] up mountains of ice. The fields where over run with water; the cattle retreated in to a house joining the ferry house off Market Street. As the water increset they got upstairs. The ice showed the house to a distance, loged on the high mountains of ice, with horses looking out of the window.

After the surrender of Cornwallis, I saw all the brass cannon, the flags and trophies of war the Americans had gained at York[*town*] from Cornwallis brought in to Philad'a by our troops. The city was illuminat on the ratification of peace between America and Britain; a triumphal arch was build a cross Market Street from the corners of Sixt Street, decorated with appropriate transparencies and splendid fireworks. I was in the pageant of the first grand federal procession in celebration of the ever memorable 4th of July 1776 in the character of Mercury, on the printer's press. Mrs. Beach [*Bache*], Dr. Franklin's daughter, made the dress, cap, and wings for me. Dr. Franklin was in the room at the time she fit the cap on my head. The dress was flesh couler, the cap and sash blue, the wings of feathers. The citizens generally partake of the dinner prepared at the mansion of [Andrew] Hammilton, Esq'r, on the hill (now called Bush Hill) near the upper ferry. In 1785 I saw the honourable body, the federal convention, set in the statehouse, with Franklin at their head, and in 1790 I beheld his funeral.

In Jan'y 1793, I saw Blanchard ascend in a boat

attach'd to a beautiful silk balloon out of the jail yard of Philad'a. He rose out of sight waveing a flag, cross'd the Deleware 16 miles in the Jerseys. Washington was present. Blanchard returned on the same day; before he step'd in to his boat, Washington walk'd up to him and gave him a letter. Minute guns where fired in potter's field by our artilary.

A band of banditti infested the country and neighbourhood near Brandyvine. They keep about the mountains, and attack travelers on the road between Philad'a and Lancaster. A woman with her daughter keep a tavern near the place. The captain of this banditti, whoes name Fitzpatrick, lodged one night at this woman's house. In the morning the captain came down to his breakfast. This heroic woman and daughter seized on the opportunity while the captain was buckling his shoes; they provided themselves with the captain's pistols. The mother presented the pistol to his breast while in the meantime the daughter tied him fast to the chair he sat in. They soon gained assistance and conducted safe to the old jail in Philad'a which stood the S. W. corner of 3d and Market Street. He was a blacksmith by trade; he broke his irons twice while in confinement. He was hung on the island in this river opposide to the city with a pirate.

About this time there was a body of French people (I expect they emigrated from Canada as they are of the same statue and complexion) who lived in a cluster of one story huts taking up the ground from Pine Street to Powel Street.

They where known by the name of the Luthern houses. The children of those people where all generally married well, and become welthy.

The first wire dancer I ever saw was one Templeman [8] who was most compleat in the art. He performed in the old Theatre South Street; the house was crowded every night. The next was a dramatic performance by Wall and Ryan [9] and Company; they had among them a Mr. Rusell [*Roussel*], a dancer. I saw him dance a hornpipe which charmed my mind. I thought I could dance as well as any body but his stile set it off, with his dress. I practised at home and I soon could do all his steps besides many more better hornpipe steps. He was a Frenchman and the French seldom do many real ground steps. The pigeon wing [10] I never saw done by any other person, and I could not make that out from the front of the house. I contrived to get Mr. Rusell to board at my father's house that I might have the opportunity to dance more correct then I had been used to. I learned the correct stile of dancing a hornpipe in the French stile, an allemande, and steps for a country dance. Except the pigeon was the only difficulty I had to encounter: he could not show me the principle and the anatomy of the figure of the step, nor I never met with a dancer since that could show it me. The mystery of the figure occured to me in bed, for my thoughts where constant on that object. I dream'd that I was at a ball and did the pigeon wing to admiration to the whole company; in the morning, I rose in the confidence of doing the step. By this strange circumstance on trial I was master of the step, and could explain the anatomy of the figure, and by a certain rule and method I never failed in teaching it and make my pupils master of it.

There was a woman in Ryans company celibrated for singing, "Tally ho." She was known by the name of Miss Hyde.[11] She sung on the South St. stage when the British officers performed in the same theatre at the time the British where winter quartered in Philad'a. A scene still remained in the old theatre within late years which was painted by Major Andre. I have been told they where all good actors.

Music and dancing was my attraction; I was noticed for my dancing. A man whose performance I would sometimes go and see exhibited in a house the corner of the little street runing from South, to Shippen St., between Front and Second St. This house is part of the oldest and the first theatre that was build in Philad'a by old Hallam and Douglass; [12] it is a large old red frame building at the corner of South and the little street, and stands there yet to this day occupy'd in tenements. This man whose name I forgot, his performance consisted of a miscellaneous collection: transparencies, the magic lantern, sea fights in machinary, singing—all bad enough, but anything was thought great in those days. As I had a mechanical genious, and a turn for music (I could play on several instruments of music), by his flattering and promises, I consented to go with him from this to Boston, on the conditions he was to pay my whole expense while I chuse to stay with him, and to give me one night's performance to my profit, and not publish my name, and pay my journey home. A desire for travelling, and in the hope of improveing myself, and gain a better knowledge of the world, I consented to go with him. This was the first and the only thing I ever done without the consent and knowledge of my father, in obedience to his will while under his command.

And now the ups and downs of my life begin. I was just in the age of 15, active, industrious, full of health and cheerfulness. I was preparing to make my first tour, to leave my father's house and mingle with the multitude of the world. My confidence in God was the security and hope in my chance of fortune; my aversion to vice, couplet with prudence, was my guide thro' life. My association was confined to partial select company; I could allways pass my time better in my chamber than in company; I was doing while some only talk of it. Idleness, resorts to taverns, low company, drinking, smokeing, gaming &c., was always my detestation. With a clear, independent spirit, I set out with this man in the stage by way of New York to Boston. In our passage we pass'd thro' (Jersey) Bristol, Trenton, Princeton (with a stately college), New Brunswick, Woodbridge, Bridgetown, Elizabethtown. From Elizabethtown point we took passage in an open boat to New York, distance 11 miles. We stop'd one day in New York; next day took passage in a packet and sailed up the East River to New Haven, took passage from there in the land stage thro' Connecticut, by way of Middletown and Harford, then thro' Massachusetts, Springfield, Worcester, and Camebridge; cross'd a flat bridge upwards of a mile long over a low water and marshy ground into Boston.

For a bout two months this man perform'd with success. He gave me a night's profit, which I saved, except a few little articles I stood in need for I bought. I also got my passage money home from him. At intervals I would be in company with a genteel young man who lived with his parents next door to my lodgings. He was a pupil of Mr. Turnner, dancing master. He introducet me in to the school, where I would often go as a spectator or visiter. Mr. Turnner had a great number of scholars of both sexes and would sometimes practice them all together when I would make sure to attend. I learned at once his method and the dances then in vogue. I saw the master's boast lay principally in hornpipes, for he would have his best hornpipe dancer dress'd in a neat sailor's dress. At a practice in the daytime my young friend was one of the hornpipe dancers. In return of friendship I taught him many steps and soon made him the best dancer in the school, by private lessons.

While I was in Boston I often visited the market, fine beef, fish in plenty, loads of poultry. An old fashioned city, streets not regular, the town uneven. From the town house runs the long warf near half a mile with stores. The vesels come up to the back of the stores and discharge their cargo. Beckon [*Beacon*] Hill is a pleasent spot. I cross'd the ferry to Charlestown. In time of the war 1776, the bridge and town was destroyed and burn'd. Since that time they have build a new bridge over to Charlestown and an elegant bridge with lamps over the marchy ground to Cambridge. I visited Bunker Hill, the first place the British attack'd. I saw on the spot, on the hill where Gen'l Warren was kill'd, the rough monument erected to his memory. I noted the inscription, and sorry I lost it. I visited the congregation of my religion. They where assembled in a very small place to worship God, but to my great satisfaction they have since built an elegant large chaple.

I took a parting glass of red wine with my young friend in the wine celler of under Dr. Cooper's church [13] (the bell of this church is too heavy to ring, but is sounded by strikeing it with a large hammer). The citizens frequent this celler and drink the wine at eighteen pence the bottle. I took leave of my young friend and set out on my journey to return home. I took the rout that leads out of Boston thro' the neck, reaching to a small town inhabited by shoemakers and weavers. From this town, I think is called Rocksberry, our cities are furnished and supply'd with what is call'd Yankey or New England shoes and whare. I bought a pair of fairtop [14] good new boots for three dollars. I journey'd on to Providence; from this I took passage in a packet to New Haven. There I took the land stage again thro' the state of Connecticut, and towns of Stradford, Fairfield, Norwalk, Stamford; (state of New York) Kingsbridge, passed the White Plains, Fort

Washington, and Fort Lee, arrived at New York, cross'd the Powlus Hook ferry, took the land stage thro' New Jersey by way of Newark and [. . .] and arrived safe in Philadelphia. As I step'd out of the stage with my small parcel in my hand, I met with an old school fellow who was rejoiced to see me. He revived my spirits by insisting to carry my baggage tho' but small and accompany me to my father's house. I approached the house with timorous steps and fluttering heart. Like the Prodigal Son returned, I entered the house, and with submissive reverence approch'd my father, who stretch'd forth his hands and with transport embraced me in his arms with a parental affection. Our tears where our substitute for words; they express'd at once a welcome and reconciliation with my father.

At this time, 1785, Lewis Hallam, Mr. Allen [15] and wife, and Mr. Moore, where performing in the old Theatre, South St., under the head of "Lectures on Heads." Mrs. Allen sung; they gave scenes of plays and scraps of pantomimes.

I had an invitation to a ball. I dress'd in costume of the times, a blue coat cut in the French stile, a white tissue vestcoat, white casemere small clothes, white silk stockings, French shoes, stitch'd heels, with small sett buckles in the knee and shoes, ruffle on the wrist and bosom; the hair full dressed with the toupee, the hair tied in a fantail club with a black rose, two curls each side well powdered; a cock'd hat, gloves, and small cane, a gold watch with gold trinkets on the chain. I attended the ball. On entering the hall,

I saw a large assemblage of ladies and gentlemen, many of my acquaintance, and here it was, the only time I ever could be prevaild on to dance a hornpipe in a private company. The next day commendation where bestow'd on my dancing thro' the city. The report reach'd Mr. Hallam's ear, who waited on my father to negotiate on liberal terms for me to dance on the stage, which with my father's consent I excepted.

Mr. Hallam wish'd me to rehearse my hornpipe in the morning on the stage, to get used to it—I expect a desire on his part to see a specimen of my talents. When I came on the stage, Mr. Hallam introduced me to Mr. and Mrs. Allen. The presence of them setting in the front of the stage to see me rehearse rob'd me of my best powers. A kind of fright seized me and weaken'd my better strength, which will allways be the situation of a novice on his first examination, especially when before such sterling old actors; you dread the criticism of their judgment. Mr. Hallam play'd the "Collage Hornpipe" on the violin. I dancet a few steps and made an apology, and hoped he would be satisfy'd, with my dancing at night. He encouraged me by assurance that he was already satisfied with the certainty that I would please. Mrs. Allen gave me a compleat discription of the suitable dress, with the advise to finish every step beating time.

The interest of the theatre principally belong'd to Hallam. Mr. Allen had a property in town, the house he lived in.

My dress was in the caracter of a sailor, a dark blue

round about full of plated buttons, paticoat trousers
made with 6 yeard of fine linnen, black satin small clothes
underneath, white silk stockings, a light shoe with a
hansome set buckle, a red westcoat, a blue silk handkerchief; my hair curled and black, a small round hat gold
laced with a blue ribband, a small rattan.

With anxiety I waited the result of the night. The theatre
on this occasion was crowded to see a fellow townsman
make his first appearance on any stage. I had contrived a
trample [16] behind the wing to enable me to gain the centre
of the stage in one spring. When the curtain rose, the cry
was, "Sit down, hats off!" With the swiftness of Mercury I
stood before them, with a general huzza, and dancet in
busts of applause. When I went off the stage, I was
encored. They made such a noise, throwing a bottle in
orchestre, apple, &c. on the stage, at last the curtain was
raised again and I dancet a second time to the general
satisfaction of the audience and managers, and gained my
point.

My dress for fancy dances was in the costume of the
celebrated dancer, Vestry [*Vestres*], in England: the coat
or fly with out sleeves made of white or colored silk, the
small clothes the same trimed with flowers or ribband,
white silk stockings, red pumps with a beau; a shirt with
French sleeves, very fine trunk sleeves from the shoulder to
the elbow, tied with a ribband in the centre, a laced shirt
collar and bosom, a silk sash and shepherd's hat to
correspond with the dress, the hair tied with a ribband. The

first thing I did in pantomime was Scaramouch in *Harli-quin Tutchstone*.[17] Mr. Hallam was the Harlequin, and Mr. Allen the clown in pantomimes, both very great.

About this time arrived Mr. Charles Busselott, a young French officer of the Lifeguard of Louis 16, a man of great ingenuity. I learn'd a great many things from him. He teach'd a fencing school in Philad'a. He was engaged in the theatre. He introduced a variety of machinary, trans-parencies, seafights, the fantasy of small shades: *Les Ombres Chinoise*, display'd by the power of light and shade. Mr. Peale [18] gave an exhibition of a phaenomenon in his old museum, the corner of Lumbard and Third Street. Mr. Busselot married my oldest sister Catharine, who sung with as much applause as I dancet. She was encored one night in the play of the *Roman Father* [19] in a song or piece of music. She was obliged to sing three times before the house could be passive reconciled.

The concern of Hallam and Allen was at an end. When Mr. Henry's company of comedians arrived from the West Indias, the theatre of South Street opened under the firm of Hallam and Henry.[20]

CALLED THE OLD AMERICAN COMPANY
Members, in their line

Hallam, in Ranger, Marplot, Epilogues, and Harle-quin.[21]

Henry, in Sir Peter Teezle, Mayor Oflaherty, and Pat-rick.[22]

Harper, in Charles Surface, Fitzroy, and Bob Akin [*sic*], and Puff.[23]

Wooles, in Capt. Bellswille, Hecate, or country esq'r, and Snuffbox.[24]

Biddle,[25] in Scotchman, sailors.

Wignell, in Prologues, Joseph Surface, and Darby.[26]

Heard,[27] in old men [. . .] and old wine.

Morris, in Sir Francis Gripe, Lessardo, Old Rowley and Sharp, and Wig.[28]

Robison, in Mr. Snake, or Careless [. . .] ⟨*and gin-bottle of rum.*⟩ [29]

Ryan,[30] prompter, occasionel actor, a good fellow.

Gay, assistant prompter.[31]

Lake, in Trip, Snake, Father Goodchild, and old fop (silk stocking and paper ruffles).[32]

Weston, master tailor, in Bagatelle, and Moses [33]—two years after this Weston turned Methodist preacher.

Snyder,[34] master scene painter.

Mrs. Henry, a great singer, formerly Miss Storace, in London.[35]

Mrs. Morris, Lady Teezle, Irish widow, and Kathleen (a favourite).[36]

Mrs. Harper, Mrs. Malaprope, Ursula, and Norah.[37]

Miss Tuke, afterwards Mrs. Hallam, ⟨*Hallam 50 and Mrs. Hallam 18*⟩ she play'd the young girls.[38]

ORCHESTRE: Phile, leader; Bentley, hapsicoard; Woolf, principle clarinate; Trimner, Decker and Son, Curtsrock; five or six more whose names I do not remember, all

Germans. Upon the whole this was a good company. I engaged with Mr. Henry: ⟨*he was very close and*⟩ he allowed but low salaries. ⟨*I have seen Mrs. Henry set in a chair in the front of the stage crying thro' passion while the orchestra play'd her music through of a song in an opera. The performers at the same time concealing themselves behind the wings.*⟩

Great exsertions where making at this time through the city to shut up the theatre. Some went about with paper to sign against it, and some for it. The company had to perform under the title of Lectures. One Shitz, the informer, brought it to a trial, and lost the cause, and was severely handled by the populous outside of the court-house. After great success, the company moved on to New York.

Previous to my leaving Philad'a I engaged our band of music and serenaded a young lady for whom I had an honourable sincere attachment. Tho' music hath charmes to melt the savage brest, to soften rocks and bend the knotet oak, yet it had not charmes enough to melt the heart of the guardian of my love who watched her so close that we could not bid farewell by the hand. The next evening I dressed myself in character of a begger and knocked at the door, to ask for some bread. While the old lady went in to get some for me, in the meantime, I gave a note expressive of my departure &c.

I went in the packet from this to Burdentown [*Borden-*

town], from their in the land stage to Perth Amboy, and there took passage in the packet to New York. The company performed in the old Theatre John Street [39] between Broadway and Nasau Street. I boarded with Mrs. Fortune [40] opposite to the theatre. The company met with good success. *The Poor Soldier* was brought out in this season and performed 21 nights. While I was in [New] York I took lessons on the violin of Mr. Phile, and of Mr. Hoffmaster, a dwarf, a man about 3 foot, large head, hands and feet; his wife of the same statue. A good musician, he composed the following hornpipe expressly for me, which is become well known in America, for I have since heard it play'd the other side of the Blue Mountains as well as in the cities.

Durang's Hornpipe
Composed by Mr. Hoffmaster, a German Dwarf,
in New York, 1785

While I remained in New York, I applied my time in the practice of dancing and music. The violin and German flute where the chief instruments I made my study. I would sometimes divert myself with the octive, the flagelet, the French horn. I made an instrument of music called Pann's pipe made of reeds, which I learnd to play so well on that I could play and dance at the same time. In the grand pageant of *Shakespear's Jubelee,*[41] I used to dance before the Comic Muse, playing on this pipe. The novelty had a pleasing effect. I applied much of my time in the study of the drama and vocal parts.

Mr. Hallam gave me some idea of the "Dwarf Dance," which by a little study I soon brought to perfection as I thought and introducet it to admiration, but I was convincet to the contrary when I repeated the dance in Philadelphia a year after. The body and the head of the Dwarf where tied above my hip, and the uperpard of my body and head where covered by a coloured paticoat gathered with my hands at the top of my head. In this concealed manner I would make my entrance. Dancing it one night I was deluded by the stage lights, which I took for the wing lights, my situation being almost blindfold. I made my exit over the spikes of the stage and orchestre. Three spikes entered my left thigh and calf, where I hung till Mr. Gibbon, our assistant tailor, extricated my leg from the spikes. I was in a swoon the whole time. I was set on my feet in the pit passage. I recovered from the swoon and did not feel my wounds but run round the theatre in to the dressing room, when I only discovered I was hurt. I was laid up two months. This mischance convinced my error, which made me make the addition to change from the man Dwarf to a woman before I quit the stage; this improvement made the dance complete. The metamorphose was from a man of 3 foot to a woman of 6 foot.

Mr. Snyder, the head painter of the theatre, lodged in the same room with me, and I improved the opportunity by practice and receiveing lessons from him in the art of painting while we remained in [New] York. The constand application in the practice of those arts confined me most constant to my room; it keep me a stranger to company, and saved me a sum of money, and enabled me to send eighty French crown on to my father in Philadelphia, and enough left in my trunk to supply my wants.

As folly indicates all young men, of which I was one of the number, my greatest frailty was in dress—rather too foppish in the street, tho' it was the fashion of the time. I would sometimes divert my mind from study—by fishing or hunting on Long Island, and in the winter, scate on the fresh water pond near the Bowery.

In the Spring 1786, after the New York theatre closed, Hallam and Henrys company lay idle during the summer, and to open the Philad'a theatre in the fall. In the meantime I returned to Philad'a to my father, full of health and spirits, and very much improved. On the second night of my arrival, I had made every arrangement, particuarly to announce my arrival, by serenadeing the young lady I paid my addresses too.

My bedroom had the appearance of a museum decorated with a great collection of paintings, a variety of instruments of music, swords and fencing foils, fowling pieces, pistols, fishing tackles, birds and squirel in cages. The curtains of my bed where contrived to festoon up or lower, by a single coard. A camera obscura [42] placed in my window, and a variety of natural curiosities.

During the vacation of the theatre, for a passtime I began to make a company of wooden actors to entertain and amuse my friends as well as myself. I made a collection of men and women, figures about two foot high, well proportioned, some model'd with paper marshea and some carved out of wood, with correct changes of charactiristic dresses, which by some information my father gave me I brought them to such perfection that my friends advised me to make a public exhibition of them. I formed my plan and entered into the execution of it, and it turned out to be a profitable income. I prevaild on my father to clear away all the partitions of the second story of his house all away. I erected a stage of twelve foot square with appropriate scenery, a curtain, with frontispiece, and stage doors, stage lamps, and chandeliers, the stage raised two foot, with an orchestre in front. The band consisted of 6 musicians; a harp was one. The seats where theatrical arranged. The whole was a theatre in miniture. I had

crowded houses every night at 50 cents a ticket. The ceiling
of the 3d story over the stage was cut away to have a quick
communication with the upper floor for a thunder loaft and
to hoist my flats strait up and down. With the assistance of
my sister who sung and spoke well, and several young men
of some talent, I performed the whole opera of *The Poor
Soldier* four nights in succession, being the first representation of *The Poor Soldier* in Philad'a. Mr. Hallam
was present and gave me flattering creadid. I trained eight
small children to perform in pantomimes and ballets. I
introduced some mechanical machinery. In shades I produ-
cet *The Magic Chamber*, or *Les Grande Ombres Chinoise*,
an antique dance by 9 dwarfs, male and female characters.

In the fall, Messrs. Hallam and Henry returned from
New York, collected their company and opened the Philad'a old theatre in South Street. In rainey weather it was
most imposible to get to the theatre within a square for
mud [and] water; yet the people would flock to it. They
where oblight to make a footway in every direction on a
wed day. One evening a rain come during the performance
and the audiance, unprepared for the mud, men and
women where obliged to wade through the mud and water
up to the calf for a square. Mrs. Bingham led the fashion to
the theatre; in short she was the star of the fashionable
ladies of Philad'a. Her castle is now turned into the
Mansion House, and the whole square was her pleasure

garden. I had the pleasure to dance twice befor Gen'l Washington in this theatre. Mr. Kenny,[43] wife, and son and wife joined the company this season.

February 27, 1787, I married Miss M'Cewen.[44] On the second night I gave an entertainment of a supper and ball to sixty of my friends. The band of music of the theater play'd during the supper and for the ball. The ceremony of the marriage was performed in the little chapple of the Catholic congregation of Philad'a by the Rev'd Father Beeson.[45]

When Gen'l Washington visited the theatre, the east stage box was decorated with the United States coat of arms over the box. Mr. Wignell, dress'd in black and pow-dered, with two silver candlesticks would wait at the box door to receive him and light him to his seat. A guard of soldiers where in attendance on the occasion, one soldier at each stage door, four placet in the gallery, with the as-sistance of our high constable Mr. Carlisle, a man of gigantic make. His dress was a black velvet coat flap waisted, small clothes and shoes all of velvet, with the old fashioned cut-silver knee and shoe buckles, cocked hat, a large black stick with the Pennsylvania coat of arms on a silver head, followed by a trusty dog. With all this pre-ventional guard, the house could not be keep in reason-able order. As soon as the curtain was down, they would throw apples, nuts, sometimes bottles, on the stage and in the orchestra from the gallery which was allways crowded, and call out for "Carlisle March," "Cherry Charlott's Jigg," "Mother Brown's Retreat," and the names of many noted characters.[46]

In the spring the Old American Company moved on to Baltimore for a few weeks and for the first time, as the success of the project was on supposition with such a numarous company, I thought it most prudent to leave Mrs. Durang in charge of her mother in Philad'a till my return. We performed in a wooden frame theatre which stood at the end of High Street and the head of the Crossway near the Bason leading to the Point. The post bills where stuck up for three successive days and each night postponed, on account of opening the doors an hour too soon. The managers took advise and did not open till dusk, after which they got good business, and convinced that the merchants could not shut up their stores so soon nor the mechanics leave off work.

I boarded at a house keep by Mrs. Gisler, a widow in High Street, old town. This wooman I shall ever respect with esteem. She was allways anxiously for my welfare. She had an ungovernable son who caused her much trouble and expense. She allways acted the part of a parent to me and my family. At this time Mr. Snyder and wife, Mr. Decker and son, Mr. Wolf, Mr. Klipstine, Mr. Ryan, and Robinson boarded in the house with me. About this time an ox was roasted in front of the courthouse, Calvert Street, in celebration of Judge Chace's election. I saw vagrants, men and woomen, working in the field of the poorhouse in the roome of horses, drawing the plow and harrow, and some at other work with spade and hoe, as a penitential punishment. Some sold at the market place for their expenses.

Here I meet with my first dancing master, Mr. Rusell, who married in Baltimore and established in a dancing school. I still keep close to my studies while I remained in Baltimore. After a short season, the company moved on to Anapolis, the seat of goverment of Maryland. The object was to perform every day in the time of the races. The races was conducted in a grander stile than I have seen since anywhere ells. The town was crowded by people from all parts, a great collection of ladies in carriages on the ground betting as well as gentlemen. It was a difficult thing to procure lodgings, so Mrs. Gisler went two days before hand, hired a house, took all her beds and kitchen furniture, and by that means still boarded us all. She took with her plenty of provision of the very best, which she allways did in Baltimore. The jaunt was for only two weeks. When we returned to Baltimore by the packets, after taking leave of my agreeable worthy neighbours, in particular Mr. Coles's family, I left Baltimore in the Frenchtown packet for Philad'a by way of New Castle, and arrived safe to Philad'a.

The theatre of Philad'a was opened for a short time. I took a benefit for the first time, and brought out the *Birth of Harlequin or the Witches Frolic*, and cleard about a hundred dollars. The business had fallen off very much. Mr. Hallam gave Harlequin, too. Mr. John Martin of New

York made his first appearance in young Norvel in *Doug-las*,[47] and was engaged. We did not remain long in Phil-ad'a, but proceeded on to New York, being a better theatrical town. However the business fell off there too, so Mr. Henry set off for England to get new actors and try what the novelty of them would produce. In the meantime we played on to very poor houses.

My journey to New York was by way of Burlington and Pearth Amboy. We experienced a dreadfull storm; the sea made up to the hatchway of the vessel as her starboard side lay in the water. The sea rushed in to the cabin windows, the woman and children in the cabin crying, every move-able thing fell topsy turvy. I felt uneasy for Mrs. Durang alltho' she betray'd no fear. Yet the situation was alarm-ing, being her first journey, to leave a comfortable home for this where hope was despair'd of. Thanks to God, and the skill of an old sea captain, we got to New York, but we where beat against other vessels and the warf before we could make a landing and that with much dificulty. I took lodging at one Doctor Herman opposide to St. Paul's Church, in the front of which is erected the monument of Montgomery. Early in the spring, I went with Mrs. Durang to Philad'a and returned to [New] York for a short time.

About this time a Monsieur Placide,[48] a celebrated tight rope dancer, and his wife, with a Frenchman called the Little Devil,[49] famous on the slack rope and tumbling, all arrived. Mr. Hallam made an engagement with them which turn'd out to advantage to the whole company. Mr. Placide was the best tight rope dancer that ever was in America. I did the clown to the rope which got me a good benefit; at least I cleared three hundred dollars, which was a great sum at that time.

Mr. Dunlap,[50] a merchant and a gentleman of property, became a third manager of the Old American Company in New York. Through him the institution keep prop'd on its foundation. Mr. Hallam was a sterling actor, but an inactive manager. His stile of acting was of the old school. He was celebrated in all the gentlemany dashing profligateness of young men, in epilogues, correct in Harlequin, and performed them with ease and spirit to a great age. He was particularly admired in Lord Oglebey.[51]

Mr. Henry was allso a sterling actor, the American Sir Peter Teezle, great in Irishman and good in operas, the best gentleman Irishman I ever saw on any stage. He was at one time an officer in the British army, and you would allways discover the deport of the soldier in him, erect and firm. He was very much subject to the gout. He usuelly came to the theatre in an old fashioned carriage; on the panel of the door he had painted a pair of crutches, with the motto, *This or Those*. Mr. Henry gave very low salaries to his performers, which keep the most of them very poor. A Mr. Biddle,[52] famous in the Scotchmen, one day turned his pocket inside out, and had wrote on it "To be Let," [and] walked thro' John St. and Broadway. However Mr. Dunlap would allways assist and advance money to a performer, and proved a great convenience and friend to actors.

Mr. Placide got up some good pantimimes and ballet dances. Mr. Placide and his wife where both professed dancers; Madam Placide occasionelly performed on the tight rope. The novelty of Mr. Placide's performance brought good houses, and made the performers good benifits.

The theatre closed with Mr. Placide; the company remained idle all summer. I returned to my family in Philad'a. I arrived at day break at Philad'a. I walk'd home with a small bag of silver dollars under my arms containing three hundred and fifty dollars. I thought myself an independent rich man. The first I meet in the street was an odd sort of a character who lived in a Quaker family. He would accost who ever he mett with pointed finger, *"I see thee first."* He saluted me with "I see thee first." He was right enough for he was the first that did see me after I landed. I had the happiness to join my family in health. Next day I deposited three hundred dollars in the North American Bank, my first capital stock, and the corner stone to my fortune—faithfully earned.

(When I first engaged with Mr. Hallam and Allen, a Mr. Tracy who followed the blacksmith's business. He was a jovial, harty sort of a man; he was noted for singing a good song in private companies. By his friends' flattery he offered to sing on the stage, and made trial, and with great applause and full houses for three nights. He sung "Bright

Phoebus" and some sailors' songs. His dress was a light blue coat, red westcoat, yellow leather small cloths, blue stocking, and buckskins gloves.)

My mind was never idle, but allways employed in some project and invention; I was not fond of an inactive life. This summer I made an engagement with Mr. Easterly,[53] the proprietor of Harrowgate Garden, four miles from Philadelphia near Frankfort. We made our arrangements adapt, and established a Vauxhall Garden, which proved to be a novel amusement to the Philad'a citizens and the adjacent country for two summers, and a profidable income to Mr. Easterly and to me. We made the calculation of our expences, and entered in the business with prudence. The entertainment was miscellaneous, the machinery and paintings done by myself. The extent of the garden was several acres of ground. With in the inclosure was a bathhouse, a fishpond, circular, runing round a small island on which stood a Chinese temple, an elegand constructed bridge leading to it over the pond, with a wast number of different discription of fish, a shower bath and a plunging bath, situateted near a long range of a forest of trees shading the lower part of the garden and baths, neat gravel walks in every direction, emballish'd by dwarf fruit trees of every discription, and chequered with elegant taste constructed summer houses. The panal beds of various flowers and rarities laid out in superb ancient style. Refreshment where supplied from the house in front and from four bars by a numerous train of waiters with the accomodation of a large yard and stabling for carriages and horses. A seperate building to hold private balls and occasionelly dinner or supper parties, elegantly furnished.

The orchestra was placed in the large prominade, being the avenue to the small walks; in a square near it was the stage. A large band of music attended. The concert commencet at 4 o'clock by a full band. The singing was performed by Mr. Kenney and his lady, and son and his lady. In the evening I had the garden fancifully illuminated in all direction with variegated lamps and transparincies at the end of each walk. In the evening the stage was well lighted, and the band moved to the stage orchestra. When my performance commenced, hundreds of spectators would visit the garden. The yard and stable crowded with horses, and carriages, and gigs.

In the winter I joined pardners with my brother-in-law, Mr. Busselotte, in management of a theatrical company. We converted a large boat builder's shop into a theatre in the Nothern Liberties and performed in it, this winter, in Front Street near the hay scales. The theatre was constructed very conveniently and handsome inside. Mr. Busselotte was an excellant painter; with my assistance we got up the necessery scenery and front of the house, wery theatrical, with box, pit, and gallery, orchestra in front of the stage. We had charactiristic dresses made to every piece as occasion required, and purchased a usefull dramatic library, a band of music.

NAMES OF THE NOTHERN LIBERTY COMPANY
Messrs. Durang and Busselotte, Managers

Mrs. Busselotte	Mr. Stuward
Doctor Vauhan	Mr. Guaran
Mr. Tobine	Mr. Pursel
Mr. Kinney	Mrs. Stuward *
Mr. Johnson	Miss Wells

* Afterward Mrs. McDonald.[54]

1793

About this time the renowned equestrian, Mr. Ricketts,[55] arrived in Philad'a from Scotland. He served his time to Mr. Hughes the equestrian near Black friar Bridge, London. He visited our theatre, on a night's performance. Next day he sent me a polite note to wait on him. I was punctuel to the appointment. He told me he was much gratifyed in seeing me dance on the tightrope, slack rope, wire, a hornpipe and Harlequin; that I would be of infinite service in a circus—and thereopon offered me an engagement, and that I was to do the clown to the horsmanship.[56] I told him I was doubtful of my abilities—in horsmanship—and there beg to decline his kind offer, which I was sorry for some time after.

At the end of our theatrical season, I opened the Vauxhall Harrowgate garden again for the second summer.

In the mean time Mr. Henry arrived from England with some good actors. Great preparations where made to open the South Street theatre with this additionel company (in Philadelphia).

Mr. Hodgkinson	Mr. Prigmore
Mrs. Hodgkinson	Mr. Floar, machinist
Mr. King	Mr. Quesnet [*Quenet*], ballet master
Mr. Sam'l West	Madam Guardie, for pantomime
Mr. James West	Monsieur Val
Mrs. Brett	Madam Val, engaged in America
Miss Brett	Monsieur Palissier [*Pellisiere*],
Mr. Robins, painter	composer of music
Mrs. Pownell	

I joined the Old American Company again. The theatre opened to great success. Mr. Hodgkinson was the best general actor that ever was, or, in my opinion, ever will be in America. He was equelly great from Macbeath down to Shelty,[58] Harlequin, or musician in vocal or instrumental. With the ease and address of a gentleman, he was admired in Macbeath, Rover, Vapet [*Vapid*] and Puff,[59] Shelty, and in the character of a sailor; his vocal powers where excellent. Mrs. Hodgkinson was a singer of a superior stile. Mrs. Pownell was a singer and actress of a superior merit; I have not seen another lady to equel her on the stage. The fascination of Madam Gardie acting was universally admired, connected with her private qualifications of an amiable lady. Monsieur and Madam Val where the first who introduced the one act petty comedy of *Pig-malion*, on the American boarde. Mr. Quesnet was a professional neat dancer from the French theatres and accumulated a fortune by teaching a dancing school in Philad'a. Monsieur Palissieur established his celebrity in compositions of music. Mr. James West was the dashing sportsman on the stage.

Mr. Wignell withdraw'd from the company and set off for England to recruit a theatrical company under the firm of Wignell and Reinagle. Mr. Wignell return'd from England and brought out a numorous company of good actors together with an extensive wardrobe and library of dramatic and musical books. Mr. Wignell and Reinagle established the new Philadelphia theatre in Chesnut Street.

In 1793 I took a lot of ground at 30 dollars yearly to pay to Thomas Willing and Robert Morris, Esq'r, with the conditions expressed in the deeds that I had the privilege to purchase the ground within the space of seven years. Fortune enabled me to buy the lot in four years' time for five hundred dollars. I have now a double house built on the lot in South Street between Fifth and Sixt Street, No. 216, which coast me, and paid for, about fourteen hundred dollars. I was the first builder on the Square when all around me was vacant, and the only one who owns the ground of their buildings in the same Square. I fenced in my lot all round and planted several fruit trees. Two apple trees bear a quantity of fruit every year. I planted a range of popler trees to shade the back of the house, south. I amused myself 3 summers in my garden, but that fell through in consiquence of my travelling. Those whom I left my house in charge with took little pleasure in gardening so all soon went to waste in the garden way.

After a successfull season in Philad'a the Old American Company moved on to New York and opened the theatre in John Street and performed to good houses. The strength of this company gave great satisfaction. Mr. Henry and wife, through indisposition and some other cause, left the stage to take a tour and are since dead. Mr. Hodgkinson became a joint manager with Mr. Dunlap. Mr. Hodgkinson raised my salary without my applying for it; it was an act of considaration and generosity and secured my esteem. End of this season in the spring, the company made up a summer scheme for the first time and devided; half of the company went to Providence, and the other half to Rhode Island. I was of the party to Rhode Island. I took my family with me. We went by way to New Haven in the packet, up the East River through a place called Hurlgate and from thence in a packet to Rhode Iland. We perform'd two months in the town hall over the marketplace, and returned again to New York and performed the winter through, and in the spring the full company went on a summer scheme to Harfort. While we stop'd here, I taught a dancing school. After a very short season the company moved on to Boston for the purpose of performing conjunctly thro' the winter with the Boston company under the management of Powell [60] and Hodgkinson.

I hired a private coach for the accomodation of my family and travelled to Boston thro' Cambridge and arrived into Boston after dark, and it was with the greatest difficulty I obtained lodgeing for the night. The town was so full of strangers that all the inns of respectibility was crowded. After a two hours' driving thro' town searching in vain to get in to some genteel house, at last I was recommended to a boarding house in the main street and centre of the town keep by a widow lady who had a number of boarders who only eat at the house: merchants, shop keepers, and clerks. This lady took me in her house with the impression that something of a profit may be made out of a family who keep a carriage and horses. After the driver had taken out my baggage, he drove off to an inn to put up his horses, which enraged her when she discovered the carriage was not mine, that if she had knew I did not travel in my own carriage she would not have admitted me. I told her in polite terms not to be uneasy on that account, that I had money enough to pay her demand for boarding or what ever trouble I should put her too. She was in some way reconciled, but put us in the garret to lodge. In the morning, the driver came for his carriage hire. I paid him 60 dollars and had a great many notes in my pocket book, which, when the lady saw, her humour changed, and ask'd me to set down to breakfast. After breakfast I went in town to look for another lodging. In the meantime Mr. King, a gentleman of our company, came to see me during my absence. She questioned him about me. He answered,

"Madam, you have got the greatest dancer in your house in America." When I returned, I prepared to move to my new lodgeings. She entreated me to stay and offered me her best room. I thank'd her and left her house. I took my family to board at an inn in a back street, the west side of the town, a very large three story brick house, sign of the Green Dragon, so weather beaten you could hardley make it out. We where put in a room up two pair of stairs at the end of a long entry. We had to pass by a spacious Masonic room. The house sounded hollow when we walk'd. Towards night it became dismal and frightful. The landlord only occupied an adjoining kitchen, and send the vituel up into our room. I stop'd but one night at this house. I at last got a comfortable room for my family with good boarding at a Mr. Jones', near the Mall, where we stayed till the company left Boston.

On Monday, December 14, 1795, the trustees of the theatre gave me an invitation to a dinner given by the proprietors at the new assembly room which joined the front of the theatre. The whole of the members of the Boston company and the Old American Company where present at this dinner, and it was here that for the first time I saw Mr. Jefferson,[61] our celebrated actor. I view'd with pleasure the reception of this stranger in our land—the feast was made cheerfull by his presence.

About this time arrived a James McGinnis and three more with him, all musicians belonging to Prince Henry's Band, deserted from Canada. McGinnis got up a grand exhibition next to the theatre, as there was no prospect to get anything by a benefit in the theatre. The managers gave me permission to perform with McGinnis on the off play nights of the theatre, which answered a good purpose to me. I got up, in machinery, the *Storming and Destruction of the Bastile*, with great praise.

Wen the theatre closed the Old American Company returned to New York. The greater part went by water. A heavey snow came on. I hired a slay with a coach body on the runner to take my family comfortable to New York all the way on the snow, thro' Providence, New Haven, and several other towns, putting up every night in comfortable lodgings.

We arrived the first and safe to New York, while those who went by water where frose in near two week. I never made money an object to debar myself or family from any comforts that was in my power to do or give, not with standing many have been pleas'd to say that I am close. The idea is founded falsly. It is because I am not seen like a good jovial fellow setting in company at a tavern prodigally over my bottle, and let the wife and children at home take care of themselves. If there is any pleasure over a bottle, let it be with a valueable friend at home, where the poor will allways find me, and not afraid to meet my creditors at my door.

This season in [New] York, Mr. Allen, Jun., son to Allen my first manager, joined the Company; allso a Mr. Marriett and his wife, Mr. Crosbye, a Mr. Nugent, Mr.

McKenzie, his first appearance in America, Mr. Hamilton and wife, Mr. and Mrs. Seymour. When the theatre closed I opened a summer theatre in Broadway opposite to the park. A Mr. Patterson once celebrated for his dancing in Ryan's and Wall's Company was with me, but I could not persuade him to dance before me. Mr. Miller, Mrs. and Mr. Rankin [62] I had too.

In 1789 I beheld a grand fate in New York when Washington was elected president of the United States. He was row'd in an elegant barge by thirteen men dres'd neatly, from Elizabethtown Point. The river was crowded with pleasure boats fill'd with ladies and gentlemen. He mounted the balconey of the fetheral hall in Wall Street, the head of Broad Street, in the mits of shouts and thousands of citizens. In the evening was display'd a splendid firework in front of the governor's house near the Battery, and the city was illuminated.

Mr. Ricketts was performing in the new Circus, Green-ege [*Greenwich*] Street opposite to the North River in New York [in] 1795. He sent me an offer of an engagement inclosed in a note. The terms where liberal with a prospect to my advantage. He would give me 25 dollars each and every week the year through and a benefit in each town, chargeing only the expences of lights, music, and advertisements. I took the affair into serious considaration, reflecting on the poor situation I held in the theatre, living on a low salary with a family, no prospect of a benefit, and on the other hand fortune appeared to invite me. I waited on Mr. Ricketts and excepted his offer; gave my managers notice of my withdrawing from the theatre. Mr. Dunlap offered to raise my salary if I would remain. I told him my mind is made up to try my fortune elswhere. I thanked him for his kind offer and the humain politeness he had always show'd me. I took my leave respectfully wishing him health and prosperity, and proud to say that it is in my power to proclaim him a compleat gentleman.

While Mr. Ricketts remained in New York, I did little else but practice on the horses every day. Mr. Mat Sully [63] was the clown in the ring at the time. Our stay was short in [New] York. We moved on to Philadelphia.

Mr. Ricketts opened his circus in Chesnut Street opposide to the new theatre in a great stile and on an extensive plan consisting of dramatic burlettes, farces, operas, pantomimes, and ballet dancing on the stage, and all discription of horsmanship in the ring.

Mr. Rickett engaged a numerous company which would have proved his ruin if he had keep them long.

THE COMPANY CONSISTED OF THE FOLLOWING

For the horsemenship in the ring was:
Mr. Ricketts, F. Ricketts, Mr. Franklin and Son,[64] Mr. M. Sully, Jno. Durang, Master Hutchins.

For the stage:
Sinior Spinacuta, tight rope dancer; Siniora Spinicuta,[65]

Columbine; Mr. Chambers, performer and singer; Mrs Chambers,[66] actress; Mr. Tomkins and his wife, Mr. Rowson, Mrs. Rowson for balletts; Miss Curry for singing and occasionel ride in the ring; Mr. Bird; Messrs. Ricketts and F. Ricketts occasionelly in pantomime; Sully in burlettes; Durang, ballet master. The pantomimes where got up under Spinacuta. We had two painters, two carpenters, a full orchestra: Leader, Mr. Lulier.

We got up the poney races which was repeated in great stile for a number of nights. We got up *The Siege of Oxetrace*[67] with great splendour and applause. The siege was performed on the stage, and the triumphal entry of Alexander the Great was lead round the ring with prisoners tied to horses' tails. The procession lead over a platform on the stage thro' a triumphal arch with all the banners, trophies, and spoils of war.

I took a benefit and had eight hundred dollars, six hundred of which I deposided in the bank. For the first time I performed on horseback. I did the clown, and keep to the horsmanship after, after my benefit.

I got up *The Battle of the Kegs*, founded on the ballet [*ballad*] of the same in the river Deleware when the British lay in Philad'a, for the benefit of Mr. Tomkins which brought him six hundred dollars in the circus. On my benefit night for the first time I sung the "Dutch Fisherman." I made a charactiristic scene in Holland of it.

Early in the spring Mr. Ricketts reduced his company, which consisted of only of himself and brother, Mr. Franklin and son, and Master Hutchins. With this small company we went to New York and opened the circus for a short time. Mr. Tomlinson occupied the lower front part of the circus where he keep the coffee room and the care of the circus during Mr. Ricketts' absence. At this time I had purchesed necessary furniture and keep house. When I left [New] York I left my furniture in the care of Mr. Tomlinson, but I never had any account of them since.

I took a benefit here and had about five hundred dollars. Mr. Ricketts proposed a new project to me, to devide the present company and each party to take a different rout. Mr. Ricketts was convincet, by experience, that a equestrian performance blended with dramatic performance would never agree or turn out to advantage, but must evidently fall to ruin. The public's taste is only to be gratify'd to see dramatic performance at a regular theatre where the manager's whole study and labour is devoted to bring it to perfection, where only an actor's merit is distinguished and rewarded. The stage holds up a mirror where the world is characteristic display'd, vice punished, and virtue rewarded. You leave the theatre with the impression of the past, and reflect on the scenes of life.

A circus within its own sphere, well regulated and conducted as Mr. John B. Ricketts established his in America, must succeed and please, and meet the admiration of the public and give general satisfaction.

Arrangements where made and our project put in practice. Mr. Rickets gave to his brother, Francis Ricketts, seven good performing horses, one of which was a white horse General Washington owned. Mr. Ricketts bought him from Robert Morris, Esq'r, of Philad'a. Those with one hundred dollars cash, with Mr. Franklin and son and Mr. Tomlinson, Jun, to start in company and try their fortune. They took the rout thro' Philad'a, Lancaster, York, Baltimore, and Anapolis and there they run aground, when Mr. John Ricketts whas obliged to send Mr. Hutchin, the groom, from Canada with five hundred dollars for their relieve, and return with F. Ricketts to Canada, after all the horses were sold by the Sheriff in Baltimore for a mear nothing before Mr. Hutchin arrived time enough to rescue them.

I took my family on to Philadelphia and settled them in my house with the convenience to draw on the bank. I deposided three hundred dollars in the United State bank and returned to New York to join Mr. Ricketts on a tour to Canada.

PART TWO

Durang's Tour To Canada

I LEFT NEW YORK the 19th of July 1797 in company with Mr. John Ricketts the celebrated equestrian hero. We engaged a convenient sloop, commanded by Capt'n Willet. We had stalls made for six horses we performed with: (names) Cornplanter (an elegant charger),[1] Lady Washington and Merry Jacko (two blacks), Governer (for still vaulting), Silver Heels (for the Tailor),[2] Little Boner (for poney races). Our voyage was 160 miles up the North River to Albany. Our company consisted only of Mr. Ricketts and myself, Mr. Leulier, a mucision, the groom, L. Bird, assistend, and Master Hutchins. Some ladies and gentlemen of New York where passengers with us. On the 2nd night of our passage in company with several sloops, I ascended a rocket near Stony Point, a hill that points to the North River on the Jersey side, terminates in small rocks to the border of the river. The fortifications in the time of the war are nearly destroyed. Here I had an opportunity to see the very house in which Gen'l Arnold and Maj'r André held their confederation on the W. side of the river; from this the artful Arnold made his escape to a British vessel that lay a short distance below; and André cross'd the river to New York side [to] meet his fate.

On the 3d evening we came up to West Point, a garrison. With in it we heard their drums and fifes and as we approach'd the fort, Mr. Ricketts, Mr. Lhulier, and myself play'd "Washington's March" [3] with wind instruments. I ascended a rocket which display'd a great number of stars. On the 4th evening laying at anchor in company of 24 sloops, some bound to Albany with passengers, I gave a display of rockets. From this, we pass'd thro' a narrow of high mountains on each side of the river, five miles long; the river narrow and the mountains so high, that men on the top look like children. When you spoke you could distinctly hear the echo of your words vibrate through the forest; it seem'd enchantment. We made a harbour every night on account of our horses, which made our voyage long, but we had provided a good stock of sea stores, fresh and salt, with poultry, wine, porter, fruit, and Spanish segars. Upon the whole it turned out to be a very pleasant passage. On Sunday we anchored opposide to the city Hudson. The Captain took Mr. Ricketts and me to shore in his long boat for the purpose to get fresh meat and garden vagitables; all we could obtain was some bread, some milk, and beans. We keep on till after dark; we struck twice on shoals, but with difficulty got clear. Several of the sloops in company stuck fast and had to wait till the tide rose again.

We arrived at Albany on Monday July 24th. The people

flock'd to the dock to see our landing. The people of those
country towns are very inquisitive; the news of an equestrian company soon spread thro' the town. After Mr.
Ricketts and myself dress'd ourselves in a neat street
riding dress, we went on shore; the groom and his assistand
landed the horses. The people eyed us from top to toe. I
judged by their sociable politeness to us that we would
meet with good success here; besides the novelty of a circus
for the first time could not fail. Our horses where put in a
stable near where we landed. Capt'n Willet invited us to his
house; we engaged to board with him at 4 dollars a week,
and found the family and every accommodation agreeable.
I took a survey of the town, while at the meantime Mr.
Ricketts waited on the Corporation, and got permission to
perform. The ground was easy obtained and we made a
temporary constructure of a circus to perform in the
afternoons, by day. The circus was divided half for the
boxes, seats elevated with a roof, the other half for the pit,
open and seats low, an orchestra, a moveable stage to
dance on, a dressing room, and stable (to dress the
horses), a low fense round the ring on which I painted
posts with a chain runing round. In a week's time all was
compleat; the first performance was on July 31st to one
hundred and sixty dollars. There was about twice the number of people out side of the building some boreing holes
thro' the board to get a peep.

My favourable opinion of the place took a turn, and
thought we would not stay long here, for I found the people

unsociable and the town dull. I observed the common mass of woman go barefoot, married or single. The original inhabitants of this place where Hollanders. They speak broken English; the girls in particular you cannot understand. You see no woman here but on a Sunday's going to church; then of course they are dress'd in their best. They are in general homely and frightened when a stranger speaks to them, but time will reform and accomplish them. There are six churches in this town, a great many taverns without custom except from strangers; about ten stages set out every day from this to other towns. I have seen more cripples and blind people in this town than any other I have been in. The sturgeon fish is a preculiar usual dish in this town, known by the name of Albany beef. I have seen the skins lay in the streets and the hogs feed on them. I saw no pumps, but a well in the centre, in the crossway of two streets with a roof over it. The streets are paved, and lamps. The square I lived, the lamps where attended by a boy who cried the hour. There is a clock in the English Church. I am informed that no business is done here but in the winter.

Saturday August 5th, in the night, broke out a dreadful fire supposed to have been set on fire in a boat builder's shop near the riverside close to our stable. It was with the utmost exertion and difficulty we got our horses out of the stable and put them in the ring of the circus in charge of the groom. Then we return'd and assisted the citizen to remove their goods. We fill'd the market house, among which was the property of Mr. Ricketts, of myself, and the family we lived with. The fire raged from 11 o'clock till 3; two hundred and 30 buildings where consumed but no lives lost. I never saw such a scene of confution; the streets full of furniture and goods; men, woman, and children runing about without clothes on, or shoes; a great many families whare left in the utmost distress and without a home. This made a stagnation in business for awhile, an end to the circus. I proposed to Mr. Rickets to give a benefit for the families distressed by the fire, and thereby enable us to take benefits. We succeeded in our plan; we had a full house for the benefit of the distressed families and put the money in the hands of the Corporation. I took my benefit and cleared one hundred dollars; Mr. Rickets took the last night, to a full house.

On Monday August 14, we all set out from Albany. In the course of the day we crossed a bridge which led over a narrow part of the Mohawk River; the landing was thro' a declivity of rocks passing thro' a rude forest. We stop'd in the middle of the day to take refreshments, and after proceeded on to put up for the night at a tavern keept by the Widow Deen. The widow gave us a good supper and provided well for the horses. She dress'd two fowls to take with us on the road the next, those with cheese, bread, porter, and Spanish segars we took with us (the Widow Deen's house stands on Sandy Hill). In the morning we took leave of the widow, and went 12 miles to a small town called Fort Ann; we could just see some remains of the fort. We stop'd at the stage house keep'd by one Griffin, and indeed a poor house of entertainment, both for man or horse. We where obliged to clean out the stable ourselves; no oats, only cornstocks, nothing to drink but New England rum, fry'd salt pork, and Bo[hea] tea, which was served up for breakfast. We introduced the widow's fowl and cheese, which set off the table better. The maid maid an appology for china cups.

After breakfast Mr. Ricketts and myself walk'd a mile and a half to a Mr. Cain who lives joining Halfway Creek or Loghouse Point. This gentleman is not idle; he has constantley an iron forges and sawmills in oporation, work'd by water falls. The buildings for his working people gives it the appearance of a small town. He politely show'd us all his works and invited us in to the house and presented several kinds of liquor. By his solicitation we stop'd and dined with him. At an early hour after dinner we made our respects to the family and return'd to the tavern. On the way met with a bridge which we where to cross over with our horses. It was broke and dangerous to cross. Mr. Ricketts and myself got some boards and rails which lay in an ajoining lot, put the bridge in some good order. We arrived at the tavern and found the groom had got all ready to start. I settled the bill with our host and we mounted our nags and journey'd on in company with two Quaker gentlemen.

On this road we cross'd a flat rock covering the breath of the road and 60 foot long. We stop'd at a tavern to wa-

ter the horses and get a drink for ourselves. On a survey
we found time had wash'd and bleached the paint off the
sign, the windows glozed with paper, the house old. We
call'd out for the landlord; out comes a man on crutches.
We ask'd him for something to drink; he said they had no
liquor, nor milk. Well, give us a drink of water. He said
the well was dry'd. O Tempora, O Moras, people who live
in cities with the advantage of full markets have no idea
of the wretched state of poverty numbers of poor families
live in, in some country parts: almost naket, shoes on the
feet would be a luxury, generally 5 or 6 children half
naket, and in this condition perhaps to go 5 or 6 miles to
a mill for a little flour for bread, &c.

At last we arrived to a town called Skeensborough, 12
miles from Fort Ann; lays at the mouth of the Lake
Champlain and surrounded by mountains, a compleat
wild looking place. The British call this place White Hall;
packets run from this occasionelly to St. Johns. We put up
at Noise's inn, a good house, the landlord and wife genteel
people. Here we found all our baggage safe in the care of
Mr. Noise, which we send on from Albany by the land
stage. We sent all our baggage from this in a packet on to
St. John's, a garrison'd town of the British. We passed
sometime in looking at some men blowing up and splitting
rocks. Here we sup'd and lodged, in the morning settled
our bill, and set out on our journey Wed'y 16 at 6 o'clock.
At 9 we got into Vermont state. A dollar goes here for 6
shillings (or, as they call it, lawfull money). We where

obliged to make a halt to put on the Governer's shoe; we always carried nails and hammer with pinchers with us. We arrived in a town called Fairhaven. We stop'd at one Rice's inn to breakfast (11 o clock); we had a desire for a good one, for we travelet over stoney roads to get one. We ask'd the landlord to let us have some poultry. He said he had no other but turkeys in the field, if he could catch one. We told him we would lend him a hand. The landlord and his son, Mr. Rickets and myself, and two boys went in the field each with a stick to knock one down. After in about a half hour we met with a flock; they took to flight, we in pursuit. The turkeys took thro' the town. Some of the neighbour began to assist; it alarmed the whole town. At last, we succeeded in catching one and Mr. Ricketts superintended the cooking of it with the landlady in the kitchen as this was his day to turn valet (we took it by turns). When occasion required to take on himself the stewardship of the day, everything was done to please us.

While breakfast was preparing two blacksmiths over-hawled and inspected our horses' feet; the townsfolk view'd our horses, a doctor of the place paid us a visit— and was very inquisitive. Mr. Ricketts entertained the docter and the landlady in the kitchen with some good stories which he would relate with such a serious counten-ance, and upon the whole they did not know what to make of us, as we never reveal'd our occupation, but when necessary. We did not get breakfast till 2 o'clock. The state of Vermont is settlet principally by Yankeys.

We set out on our journey. Our destined quarters for the night was 22 of the longest miles I ever travelet. If you ask'd anyone on the road how far it was to the next tavern, one would say it was 4 miles; meet the next, he say it was 6; none could tell. Sometimes they would first ask you, where do you come from? where are you agoing? what are you going to do with all them horses? and after that, they guess it must be about 5 miles yet. We never could get a direct answer from one. We where benighted in the mountainious desert of Vermont. After a fatiguing journey we arrived at 9 o'clock at night at an inn keep by a Squire Callender (a justice of the peace), sign of the Spread Eagle, and over the door in letters on a board, "Liberty and Equality". The esq'r appeared to be a man of few words for when he came to the door it was with difficulty to obtain a satisfactory answer from him. His wife came to the door with a candle and began to question us, and made no offer to invite us in the house. By the reflection of the candle I read the motto over the door. I thought that a sufficient invitation; we instantly put on the air of consequence and entered Liberty Hall, ordered a good supper, and oats, hay, and bedding for the horses. In the meantime we call'd in a bottle of Medeira and Spanish segars. A great change took place; two daughters of the esq'r where call'd out of bed to assist the mother in getting supper. The squire sat down with us and puff'd a segar and took a glass of wine with us. The table was set out in a handsome manner and served with a plenty of the best. He had the best liquors of all description in his celler. He has an extensive farm; every product is raised on his farm, their clothes of their own factory. In the morning we took a parting snack to the satisfaction of both parties.

I saw a great number of black squirls on this road and a half gray eagle in the woods. 8 miles from the justice's we stop'd to feed and breakfast at a place called Chimney Point at the north east side of Lake Ontario, and opposide to Crown Point, a strong Fort, on the borders of New York state. After breakfast at 12 o'clock, we set off for Bason [*Basin*] Harbour. We got out of the right road 2 miles; we cut thro' a wood for shortness, but it was thro' mud and holes above the horses' knees. We whare obliged to dismount and walk and let the horse pick their way. Ruin seem'd [to] threaten our horses. After much scrambling and anxiety we arrived at Bason Harbour on the east side of the lake; here stop'd for the remainder of the day and all night. The groom wash'd the horses in the bason. This [is] a harbour for small craft, a handsome romantic spot. The inn is keep'd by one Rogers. When we approach'd the house Mrs. Rogers, an elderly lady, stood in the door smoking a Holland pipe of two feet long, her arms a kimbo. There majestic stood fix'd till we made our obedience to her, then with the dignity of independence, and air of politeness, usher'd us into a comfortable side room. In the meanwhile the landlady was preparing our dinner, the landlord furnish'd us with some good old port and Spanish segars. The necessary orders for the horses where allways given by Mr. Hutchins, our groom, a very civil honest good man; he held a good recommandation from Aron Burr. While we sat at our wine we heard the family chaseing geese for our dinner. We prevail'd on Mrs. Rogers to dress a goose extra to take on the road with us next day, a precaution necessary in this thin settled country, to take Time by the forelock and mend the bad roads by a good meal and short stages to save the horses. Friday morning 18th we prepared to cross the ferry of a mile and three quarters wide, across the Lake Champlain; in a flat boat we sent our horses over.

On the other side we saddlet and pursuit our journey through a difficult dismal swampy woods for two hours. We made a halt 9 miles from the harbour at an inn keep'd by W. Donaughy. Two gentlemen who travelet in company with us, well acquainted with the road, served us for pilots. This inn is situated on the bank of the Lake Champlain on the west side in York state. After some refreshment we sat off to get 18 miles against the evening; but alas, we soon got into a thick wood, thro' the mountains dark and dismal, north end of York state. We could only go on a slow walk. At last we came to a small hut, and made a halt, feed our horses on corn stocks; we drank some milk, the hut full of children. On the road to this place we passed a small loghouse and saw an old gray headed man lying in a cradle smoking a pipe; a child was crying to get in. A little farther on we met another small log house and saw a man with nothing but a shirt on, the children in rags, the wife cutting wood; she run in the house. We had still 8 miles to go, the worst part of the road, through the woods and mountains, the road very narrow, the trees lofty, a succession of hills and ditches thro' rocks and mud. It began to rain, thunder, and lightning. We began to look like drowned rats. To add to our dismal situation, night came on, and of course very dark. We groped our way with the greatest care. The occurrence of wild beasts presented itself to my mind, yet I felt no fear, but placed my hope and confidence in God who I allways fear.

About 9 o'clock we arrived at a tavern, a loghouse, but a good house keep by Mr. Isac Wright, a New England man. Here we got good stables, hay, and oats, with good beds for the horses. The fireplace reached to each side of the house, a large fire, an agreeable sight. We strip'd and dried ourselves. The landlady gave us a good supper with coffee, ham and eggs, pies, cheese, fresh butter, &c, &c. The landlord made us some good milk punch before supper while we put on a change of dry clothes. Mr. Ricketts and myself had to lodge in the same bed in a room where I counted 30 whole cheeses, about 12 pots of milk, 6 large loves of bred, and some hams. This room joined the kitchen we had supper in, and served as pantry and dairy. The two gentlemen who travelet with us had a regimental bed [4] on the foor. In the morning, Saturday 19th, we took breakfast. We made an agreement with the landlord to pilot us 10 miles to the next tavern. The road was no more tractable being merely a pathway very crooket, wild, mountain-

ous, swamppy, thick wood, rocks and stones, and thinly
settlet. This path was first made by Gen'l Burgoyne; he
lead the British army by this rout from Canada into the
United States. We passed the fort where the British Gen'l
Burgoyne surrendered his whole army consisting of 5790
men to the Americans in 1777.

We set out on our journey with our guide. After two
hours' ride we stop'd at an inn keep by one Cammel. Here
we could obtain nothing to eat or drink but New England
rum and maple sugar. No bread; it is no fault of the soil,
but the indolence of those who inhabit 'em. Coming to this
place we where constantly imployed in killing large flies
that tortured our horses in swarms. Our hand where bloody
in killing so many on the neck, head, and sides of the
horses. (The following represents the exact sice.) After we

feed our horses with cornstocks we took leave of our guide
and travelet on 6 miles. Mr. Cammel hired us a horse for
one quarter dollar to carry our baggage 6 miles and let him
loose to return home himself. We arrived at Plattsbourgh

at 5 o'clock and had dinner on the table at 8 o'clock in the evening. Our horses where well provided for. While dinner was preparing, Mr. Ricketts and myself took a survey of the town. Plattsbourgh is pleasently situated close on the shore of the Lake Champlain. The Surranic [*Saranac*] River runs through the town and empties in to the Lake Champ'n. The town is called after Esq'r Platt, Sen. A mill was building at this time for young Esq'r Platt on the river, near a bridge which is constructed across this river. The inn we stopt at is keep by a Mr. Green, a good house of entertainment. There is a large public building appropriated for three purposes, for divine service, courts of justice, a prison, besides the market held undernethe. As Mr. Ricketts and myself walked over the bridge we saw a crowd before the door of a small tavern on the hill. As we approached nearer we discovered the assemblage to be composed of the inhabitants who, after their weakly labour, collected in a neighbourly sociable jollyfication, which is common in country towns on a Saturday afternoon. We met with a young gentleman from York, who was in possession of some property here. Two gentlemen who stood spectators on the hill advancet to meet us. One was young Esq'r Platt, a other a doctor. We where introduced to them by our friend. We invited them to take some porter and segars with us. After our dinner, which was about 9 o'clock, we spend the evening agreeable, and we walk'd to the bridge at a late hour to see the inhabitants fishing for salmon trout with torches made of pine knots.

One man sets in the front of the boat with the torch, while another with a harpoon is on the lookout and stabs them. I counted 24 torches. They sell the salmon for twopence a pound.

On Sunday morning the 20 we took breakfast. Salmon was served up. The lady of the house waited on the table; she gave us some nice chacholate; on every cup she greated nutmeg. After breakfast we took our leave with many cerimonies. We sent what baggage we had with us in an open boat to St. Johns. 3 miles on the road we stop'd to deliver a letter to a Mr. Threatwell. So far the road was good, but for the remainder of the road we had to encounter was bad enough, and without a pilot. At 5 miles farther we stop'd for the day at an inn, keep'd by a Mr. Dailey—this place is called Rush [*Rouses*] Point—close to the shore and facing Lake Champlain, a good house for entertainment. Mr. Dailey kill'd a lamb on our account. In the mean time Mr. Ricketts and myself caught a mess of fish in the lake which we had dressed. With a quarter of the lamb, some ham, pies, custards &c., Mrs. Dailey set out the table with credid. Two bottles of porter we brought with us, and some of the good chocholate for our breakfast next morning.

On Monday 21, after breakfast, Mr. Dailey piloted us 10 miles through as bad a road as we had traveled yet, sometimes thro' swamps then over mountains—then thro' a thick woods, then for a long part of the way on the beach sinking in the sand—the sun scorching, and the flies biting

—on the west side of Champlain. On this rout we pass'd
some log houses, some covered with bark of trees, some
with no cover; they are inhabited by Canadians. At last we
arrived at an inn keep by one Douglas: good entertainment
in the house, but a dirty yard and no stable. We made a
short stay here. We engaged a man to pilot us to our next
destination, and but for his knolage of the rugged narrow
pathway we where torn by the limbs and briers, the horses
in danger of brakeing their legs between the roots of trees.
At last we arrived at the wish'd for spot. We crossed a
bridge and dismounted at the door of a Judge Moore. We
took it for an inn, finding no sign of a tavern in the place
which is called Sharecee [*Chazy*]. 3 houses made up this
town. There was no alternative left but the painful ne-
cessety of making an appropriate apology and solicit a
night's lodging for us and stable room for our horses, when
at the same time we had plenty of money to pay our way. It
was a delicate point to the feelings on booth sides. Mr.
Ricketts took the task on himself in most polite terms with
the air and spirit of an accomplish'd man of fortune. He
succeeded to unbend the stern brow of the judge to a
hospitable invitation; what he had, was at our service. The
horses where put in his stable and supplied with oats and
hay. Mrs. Moore treated us in a genteel manner, but the
groom and boys where obliged to sleep in the stable and do
without supper, and thrash out the oats. The esq'r gave us
some rum and water. He once followed the tailoring
business in New York. The lady made tea for us with some

preserves. He shewed us to a small bed room joining his on the same floor. Being quartered on charity, we whare as still as a mouse all night. The esq'r owned a deal of property on this spot, saw and gristmills. A party of Indians arrived at the judge's this afternoon to receive they [*their*] pay allowed by the New York state. This being the line between the United States and Canada, [there are] many Canadian and New England people. A portion of land is given free for a term of years without tax to each family to cultivate it, and, if very poor, tools found them. In Canada the King claims only the public roads and garrison'd ground.

Tuesday: 22d. Early in the morning I offered the judge pay for our fare but he politely declined to take anything. We took our respectful leave and took with us a Canadian to pilot us through the woods by an Indian pathway. He refused to ride, but went on foot before us for 35 miles. The groom and boys where very hungry having no supper the night before or breakfast this morning. I perceived a cottage at some distance; I went to it and saw none but two children. There where two loves of bread on a table. I took one and put in the place a dollar, and gave the bread to the groom and boys.

We travelet on very slow, scrambling through a subterraneous forrest. Sometimes we jumpt the horses over fallen trees, and let the horses pick their way over the roots of trees. The boy [was] brush'd off his poney in a shower of rain. Now and then we would meet an Indian, sheds made by Indian hunters. I saw large trees with a square piece of the bark taken off and the figure of a deer or bear carved on it by the Indian who killd it, and let the game lay by the tree, and assured it was safe till their wives brought it away who knew their husband's mark. We travelet for sometime in the night and passed two Canadian villages; no other language was heard now but French. About 9 o'clock at night we arrived at a village called La Tortie [*La Tortue*].

We put up at a Captain Pomroy, a private French house, the stable bad, but the best hay I ever smelt, and good oats. In the course of a conversation with the Captain I drop'd a hint about supper, for we had not eat anything the whole day. The Captain had lent Mr. Ricketts and myself some clothes to put on while we dried ours. In the meantime they placet on the table a large earthen dish of milk and two spoons. Mr. Ricketts wished to eat his milk in a seperate dish. They brought him a large wash bason out of which he eat his milk and bread. A large brown loaf was on the table. They brought me a white chamber bowl with the handle broke off, which the family use themselves for an eating dish, so I made myself contended. The whole family sat round the table looking at us. After we eat, we smok'd segars which excited their curiosity still more, as they only smoke short pipes of about two inches long. We presented the Captain with one, who smoked very aukward to the great diversion of the family. The appearance of the Captain reminded of Blackbeard; he was a low figure, stout, and like an old black beard Spaniard, his wife young, about six foot, thin and spare, dressed in a short linsey [5] paticoat reaching only to the calve, blue stocking, high heel slippers, a tight lacet linsey body, a small red handkerchief, black hair done up very snug, and a calicoe cap or headpiece; both dark complexion (so are all the Canadian, and squatty statues) and calicoe aprons. Mrs. Pomroy laid herself before us right across the table with her arms folded, gaping in her husbands mouth while smoking. There were only two large rooms and on the same floor; the one we eat in was the kitchen and eating room, the other was their bed room. At supper the Captain lent his pocket clasp knife for us to cut bread. I saw no knives or forks. Every Canadian carries a pocket knife to cut his tobacco and bread.

The Captain showed Mr. Ricketts and me into his bed room to a bed prepared on the floor for us in the opposide corner to his own. The door was left open, or I believe there was no door. The family still looking at us, we did not like to undress, so we pull'd off only our coats, west, and boots, and lay in bed. Very soon the Captain came in and went to bed with a large stripe woolen cap on and let the candle burn. Soon came in his wife with a cradle under her arm with a child in it. After putting the cradle down, she threw herself across the bed and kiss'd the Captain. Mr. Ricketts and myself had to smother our laughing by putting the sheet in our mouth to witness the scene between old Neptune and his Amphitrite. At last she undressed, blew out the candle and went to bed. In about an half an hour 6 or 8 reapers came in the other room, men and women. After eating something, [they] made a regemental bed with buffalo skins on the floor, and all lay down to sleep in sight of us. The groom and our boys slep in the hay loft. As for our parts, we did not sleep the whole night. The Captain had not delicacy enough to prevent natures report, every now and then, being the signals of wind. Upon the whole this was a scene of rustic simplicity.

Wedesday 23d. In the morning I ask'd the Captain what we had to pay him; he left it to us. I gave him a few dollars and he was well satisfied and went with us part of the road, and beg'd if we came that way a gain to stop at his house.

We found this journey of 6 miles to be very pleasent, a very level road, the country thickly settlet by Canadians. At every mile on the roadside stands the figure of a Cross, annexed in a group: the nails, a ladder, a rope, the thorns, a speer, a whip, a sponge, all carved, are placed in the center of the Cross, and a small distance below is a niche sunk with a glass over it which contains a crucifix, and all who pass or meet it make a reverence to it. At 11 o'clock we arrived at an old fashion'd town called La Prairie. We put up at the coffee house keep by Lafeevre, a Frenchman. After dinner Mr. Lafeever furnished Mr. Ricketts and me with a calash and horse, which we call horse and chair in the States, and drove 18 miles to St. Johns to receive our baggage, which came to this by water from Whitehall. Our horse crawl'd on so slow that we where obliged to stop one mile this side of St. Johns, and in the morning (24) we walk on foot into St. Johns. We took breakfast at the principle inn keep by Mr. Cheeseman, where we found all our baggage safe and entered at the Customhouse. Mr. Ricketts was obliged to go to the guard house of the garrison to enter or give in the names and occupation of his company and baggage, with the object of his business, which was accomplished with satisfaction. We returned to La Prairie after we had sent off our baggage in a wagon.

We got in La Prairie at 4 in the afternoon and lodged here this night. In the morning, Friday 25, after breakfast, we crossed the ferry from this, being 9 miles across the River St. Lawrence to Montreal. We put our horses in two flat bottom'd boats, arrived at 12 o'clock in the suburbs. We put up at an inn keep by Simon Clark, a New England man, but long in the employ of the British as interpiter to the Indians and lives near the Recollet Gate within the city wall.

On Monday 28th, Mr. Ricketts obtained the ground for the circus belonging to the King. It was situated in a corner of the rampart, near the Recollet Gate guard house. I laid out the circus in a drawing for the carpenters and mark'd out the skeleton of the circus. It was build without a top for day performance. In two weeks it was compleated with ring, stage, dressing room, and stables. The house was devided, a row of boxes elivated, and the pit underneth, with a coffee room. The 5th of September we opened.

We performed every afternoon at 4 o'clock, the band of music belonging to the 60th Regiment, Royal American Grenadiers. The labourers of the circus where soldiers off of duty who work'd at a half a crown a day, and that was the salary we gave the band. Mr. Gillis was the leader. Mr. Ricketts of course was the head and principle performer in the equestrian line, and to his credid the best that ever was in America. My business was the Clown on foot and horseback, and obliged to furnish all the jokes for the ring, and to ride the Tailor to Brentford, with the dialogue which I was obliged to speak in French, German, and English (the principle inhabitant are French, a great many Germans, a few merchants, and British soldiers English).

I rode the foxhunter, leaping over the bar with the mounting and dismounting while in full speed, taking a flying leap on horsback through a paper sun, in character of a drunken man on horsback, tied in a sack standing on two horses while I changed to woman's clothes; rode in full speed standing on two horses, Mr. Ricketts at the same time standing on my shoulders, with master Hutchins at the same time standing in the attitude of Mercury on Mr. Ricketts' shoulders forming a pyramid. I performed the drunken soldier on horsback, still vaulted, I dancet on the stage, I was the Harlequin in the pantomimes, occasionelly I sung a comic song. I tumbled on the slack rope and performed on the slack wire. I introduced mechanical exhibitions in machinery and transparencies. I produced exhibitions of fireworks. In short, I was performer, machinist, painter, designer, music compiler, the bill maker, and treasurer.

The Canadian inhabitants thought our horses where supernatural, that it was impossible horses could dance and keep time to music, that the man dancing a hornpipe on the saddle while the horse was in full speed; Mr. Ricketts was very great in that. We where the first equestrians that ever was in Canada, therefore the Canadian inhabitants where ignorent of the science and thought the whole a conjuration. However, so far they were right that a horse can not keep time to music—we allways adapted our music to keep time with the horses. They soon where convincet that we are like other people, and much pleased with us.

Mr. Ricketts received such encouragement from the merchants and officers to remain the winter thro', in four weeks we shut up our summer circus and began to finish this on a more permanent one. We where compel'd to build the circus of stone all round, and put on a roof with sky lights, a coffee room. The circus was constructed in the inside the same as the Philadelphia circus: the box elivated, the pit in the front on the ground floor, our dressing rooms and satle [settle][6] where underneath of the box floor, a large stage orchestra over the door where the horses entered. I painted the inside myself. The doom was a light blue sky colour, cupids bearing garlands of roses round the circle, the boxes rose pink, pannels white, with a festooned blue curtain, the ring in panels intersperset with posts and gold chain leading round. The stage department was decorated with scenery, a curtain, a frontispiece, stagedoors, a niche on each with busts of armory. We performed *Captain Cook, Robinson Crusoe,*[7] Harlequin pantomimes, and ballet dances.

Mr. Ricketts and myself made a visit to an Indian village 3 leagues from Montreal which lies on the S. W. side of the St. Lawrence. Mr. Ricketts was in an Indian's dress which he sometimes rode in. We left our colash and horse at an inn in the village called Lashine, N. E. side, and cross'd the ferry over the St. Lawrence, about a mile wide. We had a recommendation to visit a Captain Tommoa, an old Indian warrior of 76 who keep a house to entertain strangers in the village called Cochnewago [*Caughnawaga*] inhabited entirely by Indians. He received us with great respect and pleasure. He showed us into a side room well furnished and gave us some good old port; he had all kinds of the best liquor in the house. He told us that he did not sell a drop to any of his towns people, only to travellers, nor not a drop of liquor could be had in the town but at his house. It was forbid, to keep the Indians sober. He furnished a good dinner. He was the richest man among them and the only one dress'd in modern clothes, sometimes in British uniform and cock'd hat. His wife and family where dress'd in the compleat Indian costume: a short blue cloath paticoat, red leggance, mockasons, a calicoe short gound, draw'd at the neck or rather fastened by silver broaches, her black hair platted at

each side hanging down from the temple, the hind hair tied
and platted, hanging down fastened by a silver ring. She
appear'd to be a domestic woman. While we where at dinner
in the parlour, the captain and his family sat down to their
dinner in the kitchen. He came in the room occasionelly
and very attentive; he ask'd us if we had any curiosity to
taste the dish which they made their dinner of. We beg'd he
would gratify us; he brought in a dish of beans and Indian
corn—this was the first time I ever eat homony. Then he
show'd us his bed room. They lay on boards raised from
the floor with a blanket only, or buffalo skin in the winter.
A child was tied on a board wrapt all over tight till up
to the neck and fastened round with strings made out of
buffalo skins; the child was stood up in a corner of the
room.

In the afternoon Capt. Tommoa invited a bout a dozen
chiefs of the town and introducet us with no other ceremony but a shake by the hand. Some of them could speak
French and that was the only tongue in which we could
convers with the captain. The chiefs took their seats in a
formal way round the room and after drinking some
punch, porter, and wine some of them sent for their
daughters, who where all young, neatly dress'd, some
handsome and well shaped. They performed a dance with a
most reserved modesty, by couples behind each other. They
moved on slow with only one simple step, something of the
clesade [*glissade*], their countenence an innosent down
look, quite erect in their whole person, their arms strait

down by the side, all keeping an exact time to their music, which was play'd by an old chief beating one stick against the other (being a substitute for a drum which they use, made out of the body of a tree, a bout the sise of a small cask with a skin stretch'd tight on the top). Those girls would move in Indian file and strait line to right and left and meet again, then lead off to right and left in Indian file, round and meet at the bottom and join their pardners as before, with a repeat of the same, gracefully. They did not fling their arms and legs about as I have seen ladies do at our balls.

After the dance, Captain Tommoa accompanied by some of the chiefs took Mr. Ricketts and me to visit the grand chapple of this town. Passing through the streets the chiefs introduced us to their families. Many of the Indian huts are very comfortable, but the most of them very miserable—a ground floor, all one story, and live in one room only. I saw a great many women and men laying before the door in the sun with a blanket round them. I was charmed to admiration when I entered the chapple to behold an edifice like this in an Indian village. The chapple is a large stone building. The decorations inside are superb, a large well furnished altar and on each side of the altar in the front standing perspective are the twelve apostles as large as life carved out of wood. When an Indian commits any offense or been drunk, he is doom'd to set outside of the chapple door in the time of service as a punishment. After we left the chapple a group of young

Indians performed several games to entertain us, after which they prepared their canoes and padlet us a cross the river to Lasheene. After we landed, I stay'd with them while Mr. Ricketts went up to the inn and set them down a jug of rum.

We returned in our colash to Montreal, on the way passing a mill. The miller, a fine fat jolly looking man, call'd to us and invited us into his house, as he told us for the purpose to show us how a Canadian miller lives. He introducet some wine, ham, bread and cheese, which made it night before we got to the city.

When the hunting season of the Indians are over they come to Montreal to sell their game, and other things which their squaws make for market (in hunting they use riffles). The Indian will come in town 3 or 4 at a time walking indian file. In about a quarter of an hour you'll see their squaws carrying the burden slung with a string made of bofalo skins round their shoulders or forehead, and perhap a child tied on a board hanging on the back. In the market they'll hang the board suspended by a string with the child on it on a nail, hook, or any place convenient, or stand it in a cornner.

In this manner the Indian gether to a wast number. After selling their marketing, they'll get drunk and lay about the streets. I saw a large assemblage of them before Mr. Clark's door commencing a compleat Indian frolic. Clark was obliged to shut his house up and so did the neighbours. They began to give their yells of horror, hoops and shrill shrieks, their antic struts, flourishing their tommohawks and boasting of their exploits. In the hight of this fun, if they owe one an old grudge, it is now revenged. They strike all through each other. The women generally keep sober, knowing their way and alternation, rush between them, and take away their knives, and endeivor to passify them, and receive many a blow aim'd at their opponent. They will [stab] each other, and by the time the affray is half over they'll most all be start naket. A young Indian stabs his sister for a scandel she had brought on to his family, and some time before he stabs the man who had been the cause, and no notice taken of it.

I could not stay any longer in Clark's house as his yard joined the barrack yard. Every morning they flog'd some of the British soldiers. It became disgusting, and I removed my lodging to a private house keep by a Widow Kinsler, a German woman in the St. Lawrence subburbs near the circus, where I had a room with a stove, a bed with curtains. Her son, John Kinsler, slep in the room with me; he eat with me and waited on me at home and at the circus. He was a very obliging good fellow. Here I made all the chandeliers, drapery, moveable machinary, and fireworks for the circus. I boarded here for one dollar and a half a week, and good living.

I purchased a Canadian horse, one of the best I could find, for thirty dollars. I never neglected going to chapple of a Sunday. The chapples in this country are very grand. The chapple of Montreal has three altars; the ceremony of the service is performed with greater splendour than I ever saw anywhere else. I counted fifty priests in front of the altar. I saw the Bishop in his full vestment consecrate the new flags of a regiment.

I was several times invited to dine and sup with some respectable citizen families, in particular at Mr. Jonas. His lady had a method of cooking fish better than I ever tasted anyware ells. A French doctor invited me to dinner, and hoped that if I should brake a leg or arm, or any other accident should happen in my performance, to give him my custom.

On the 31st of September the new circus was finish'd. We performed to good business for a while. When it became slack, I advised Mr. Ricketts to give an ox to roast on the River St. Lawrence. The novelty of the thing brought a crowd to the town. We performed on the same evening (January 1st[?], 1798). The house was crowded. The butchers march'd with a band of music thro' the town with gold letters on the horns, "God save the King," which did the business and paid Ricketts well.

I went with Mr. Kinsler to a French wedding about a mile in the country. In a small room where about forty people a dancing, old and young, nothing to drink but a bucket of water in a cornner and tin cup. Two would dance a minuet in the space of a small table; they keep it up for three days and three nights.

Mr. Ricketts had a desire to see the inside of one of the convents. I advised him to give a benefit night profits to them and that would be a good introduction. He agreed. We advertised a benefit for the convent that stands near the Recollet Gate; about one hundred and fifty dollars was presented to them. In about a week after, Mr. Ricketts and myself went to the convent and gave in our names to a porter who attended the outward door. The lady abbess, a portly good looking lady, came into the hall to receive us. She had all the manners and accomplishment in her address and conversation of an elegant bread lady. Her familiar ease announced her character at once. She invited us to see every appartment. She showed and explained the whole situation and institution to us. She was accompanied through the building by several young nuns. She showed us the chapple of the place, the hospital room, a room where many nuns where at work in embroideries and all kind of needle work. We thanked her and took our leave respect-fully.

The snow lies very deep here so that it covers fences, ditches; the river is covered in such a manner that you cannot distinguish it from the land. The slaying is very bad on account of the pesentry's slays on low runners which gether so much snow in the front as to cause every 20 feet a hill, which they call cowhoos, and slays they call carryalls. I bought a slay which was the [. . .] of a peacock from Simon Clark for a half joe.[8] I painted it up a fresh. Mr. Kinsler and myself tryed my new horse in it. We went 15 miles, to a French village, all the way on the river St. Lawrence, to this village called Le Varene [*Varennes*] on

John Durang in character of the Dwarf Metamorphosed

Road to St. John. Cross on the left hand

Cap Saunta Chapple. Road to Quebec. Chapple stands on the right hand

John Durang in character of a Hornpipe

John Durang in character of the Dutch Fisherman

Mrs Sr Durang in Character, of a Highland Fling. Ballett of Auld Robin Gray.

John Durang in character of a Highland Fling. Ballet of Auld Robin Gray

Mrs. J. Durang in character of Harlequin. Animation Scene, in five positions.

John Durang in character of Harlequin.
Animation scene, in five positions [*in fifth position*]

John Durang in character of a Pas seul à Vestris

the east side of the river. It has a fine chapple with three steeples and two bells. We ment to return the same day, but a heavy snow storm came on, followed by rain, so we concluded to remain all night. In the morning it still was the same weather. As it was play day and my absence, together with a report in the city that we had broke in the ice and drowned, gave Mr. Ricketts much alarm. He sent people after us who we met on the road, for I ventured thro' the storm as I knew my presence was necessary to be at the circus.

I arrived late in the afternoon and we performed that night. The roof of the circus leak'd and was very wet. In riding the Tailor, the horse's legs slipt from under him and he fell flat on his side with my leg under him. I escaped the misfortune of breaking it, but my knee swelled very much —after which I dancet a hornpipe to show the people I was not hurt. Yet the next day I was lay'd up and for three days. An old French doctor lady cured me; she also cured a woman of a cancer in the breast by applying live toads to the part affected. They sucked the poisoness inflamation from the breast and cured her.

The circus stood at the west end of the parade ground. Every afternoon at 4 o'clock they made a handsom parade with two regiments, the band of music on an elevated orchester opposide to the soldiers. The drums and fifes would come in a group from the barracks and enter the parade at the north end. The parade always closed by fileing off to their different barracks. The band of music remained on the ground to entertain the officers and genteel inhabitand; it was altogether a hansom appearence.

The costume of the Canadian men is a capude, a kind of frock coat laps over to the side and reach above the knees, with a hood fastened to the collar behind, a santuery or sash round the waist, coars, coloured small clothes, woollen colour'd stocking, mocosens in the summer and wooden shoes in the winter. (I bought a pair of wooden shoes at market which the peasent bring in at 12 pence apair.) They generally wear a coloured woolen cap, the neck open, and a pipe in the mouth of about 2 inches long. They are of a low statue, dark complexion, a cheerfull hardy sort of people. The Canadian woman dress of a Sunday in a white or mostly in a calicoe paticoat, some in a coloured stuff, a lacet coloured jacket, and calicoe cap and apron, the girls in calicoe, shortgown'd. They go with their pardners to church and in the afternoon they'll dance. But in general the Canadian peasentry live very poor, yet the poorest will have curtains round the bed. In the winter I have seen the peasants come to market with their produce in a small slay drawn by dogs. Some bakers in the city use dogs to carry their bread about. When a Canadian comes into a house, he talks with as much spirit as if he was an independend liver, yet perhaps he is poorly off at home. I have been told by a Canadian that sometimes they eat mice. I have been told Canada raises two crops of wheat a year. I saw a great many maple trees from which they extract their sugar; they bore a hole near the bottom, put in a long peg, it will run out of that and received in a tray or trough made out of part of a tree, and after boild, and framed in long squar lumps and sell at market at 6 or 8 cents a pound. I bought one of their best turkeys for a quarter of a dollar.

At the interval of our performance we gave lesson to ladies and gentlemen in riding and broke several horses for the officers.

Voyagers are listed here by Messrs. McTavish and Forbisher [9] for the fur trade to upper Canada. It is a novel sight to see them set out; each man carries his share of burden, and so many allotted to carry the boats when they go over land. And when paddling in the water, one of them will sing a voyager's song and all join the chorus.

Bufoloe skins are generally used on beds in the winter, some parts of the country mountanious, but the road mostly very level, keep in order by the peasants as that is the only tax they pay.

Before we closed the circus I took my benefit. I brought out on my night an English comedy of two acts called *The Ghost.*[10] Collonel McIntosh gave me his band of music with the promise to do every thing in his power to make me a good house, which he did. The band performed the characters in the comedy; I did the part, Clinch. I got up an Indian characteristic dance. The N. Wst. Company lent me Indian clothes for those concearned in the dance. I had my own dress which I purchased from an Indian for rum. The dances I learned from some Chipeway and Naudowessie chiefs of the West. My dress was most compleat with chichicoes tied round below my knees (a kind of large dried bean hollowed and strung, make a music to keep time like the castinates). I performed the *Pipe Dance;* the manner is gracefull and pleasing in the nature of savage harmony. Next, the *Eagle Tail Dance.* I concluded with the *War Dance,* descriptive of their exploits, throwing myself in different postures with firm steps with hatchet and knife, representing the manner they kill and scalp and take prisoners with the yells and war hoops. I was told by the officer that I excel'd as their native Indian dances where more simple. I jumpt thro' a barrel of fire and concluded with an exhibition of fireworks. I had eight hundred dollars in the house. Soldiers off of duty marched in companies in to the pit, the habitants where showed [*shoved*] in the ring, and when the horsemanship went on, obliged to retreat on the stage.

Before we closed, I visited Montmorency 13 leagues northest of Montreal. I heard the falls roar two miles before I arrived to the spot. There is a kind of summer-house build out facing the falls to have a view. 75 steps lead from the top of the surface to a platform at the bottom. It is a grand and awful sight; the ice makes a terrible work when the river brake up: rocks of ice shoved mountain high.

The last night of performance in Montreal May 3d 1798. On Wednesday morning, May 9th, I set off in company of Mr. Francis Ricketts, the groom, and two boys in charge of the horses. Mr. John Ricketts stop'd behind to settle. After we got some part on the road, I turned back to settle some accounts of my own which I had forgot, after which I pursuet my journey again, but I did not over take them this afternoon. I was overtaken with the rain, and put up for the night at a village call'd Point Tramble [*Point aux Trembles*] at an inn keep by Donagany, lying on the shore of St. Lawrence. Several market boats where obliged to stop here all night on account of the weather. They sung, told stories, drank water, and eat bread to their great diversion. In the morning on Wednesday 10th, I set off at five. About a half a league off, I was caught in the rain again for a short time only. I crossed a very bad ferry which took up about an hour and a half. At 10 o'clock I stop'd at a farm house. I had nothing but gold in my pocket which they could not change so I had to do without breakfast. I went on with speed to over take young Ricketts. At last I made out the track of our horses' hoofes, which I knew by the ponys. I followed the track down a bye road towards the river, a small village called St. Sulprice. The town consists of a church and two houses. My folks where just at breakfast and rejoiced to see me. Here I took breakfast. The landlord changed me a half joe and we set out on our journey again. On the road we came to a small house with some people collected at the door. Presently came a man on horseback in full speed ringing a large bell, a Roman clergyman in a chair following —he was call'd from the next village to a man on his death bed. At 5 o'clock we arrived at a small village called La Birtia [*Berthierville*]. We stop'd at an inn next door to the Roman clergyman we met. I can't say much about this inn as all Canadian inns are mostly a like, and have no signs. We lodged here all night and in the morning, Friday 11th, 7 o'clock, we where ready to start. This clergy gentlemen politely told us that it was imposible to go by the post road as the bridge was carry'd a way, but directed us in a by road which would take us 3 leagues out of the way further to the next stage house. There was no choice but this left. We went on and forded a creek up to the horses' bellies. At 12 o'clock we stop'd at a place called Masgeuronge [*Maskinonge*]. We breakfasted at here at the post house. Here we got a drink of beer which a merchant had to sell. We left this place at 3 o'clock and went only two leagues further to a small town called River Delue [*Riviere du Loup*]. We stop'd at the post house, and they had nothing for man or horse.

We where oblight to cross a long bridge and put up for the night at a private house. The man of the house is a farmer by day and a cooper at night and the house stands close on the River Deloup from which the town has taken its name. These people gave us the use of their house and barn, but very ill provided to entertain travellers. We where obliged to buy our oats and some tea sugar for our supper from a merchant on the west side of the bridge, and in the evening he paid us a visit. We got some good brandy from that gentleman. I ask'd the lady of the house

what she could give us for supper. She had nothing but
bread, milk, cheese, and some duck runing in the yard. I
told her she would much oblige us to kill two ducks and
make our tea. After we had smoked a segar and took a
drink, a black lady entered the house in great stile. She
was dress'd in a blue riding habit, black hat and feathers,
a whip in her hand, gold watch, gold chain and locket
round the neck, lacet boots, a red satin under west, her
figure tall, slender, and well shaped. She had a polite
address; she talk'd very familier and ask us where we
come from and our business. We told her that we had
dispatches from the United States goverment to the British
goverment. She made her exit with a swiming courtsey;
who she was I know not. By this time supper was on the
table, but no tea cups nor teapot, for our obliging landlady had boild the ducks and tea in one pot, and sarved
up in a large earthen dish. So we where obliged to make
our supper on milk and bread and cheese. Good enough
for a hungary man.

Saturday, 12. We set off from this at 6 in the morning;
by 9 o'clock we had got 3 leagues off to a place called
Marchicha [*Yamachiche*]. We took breakfast here and
started at 3 o'clock in the afternoon. We arrived in the
town called the Three Rivers. Here we meet with the best
house on the road and of course the dearest—and cheepest
in the long run. The house is keep by one Arnotty. He
keeps a good house of entertainment; here we got a drink
of beer. This is a handsome little town; the best building is

the barracks. There are a great many nuns here who make all kind of needle work and bark work to sell. I bought several articles.

Sunday morning, 13. We set off at 7 o'clock. A bout one league from Three Rivers we crossed a wide ferry over the river called Suverre River, but it was with difficulty and risk [in] old flat bottomed battows. We took two horses at a time, which took up two hours. One league further we stop'd at a place to breakfast, a small village called La Twa Riviers. A good house in keep here; a handsome place of worship called St. Mary's Chapple. From this, we crossed two ferrys more and put up at an inn close on the other side of the second ferry, and a very good house for entertainment. We had supper and lodgings for 4 and oats and hay for 7 horses and only had to pay 11 shillings.

Monday morning, 14. We set off at 7. About half a league off we crossed a ferry over the River St. Mary and just on the other side on a rising ground stands as beautiful a Roman chapple as ever I saw in the United States. Some little distance off on the road I saw the priest of this chapple with his congregation walking in procession with banners, and all the church's ceremony, performing service at the same time, walking slow in procession through the village. (Half a league further we stop'd to refresh. The post houses are clean, well provided with good bed, but a few of them have but little to eat—here is a fine country, but the people too lazy to help themselves, like the Indians.) After we cross'd the river and came up to the chapple, I bid young Ricketts to go on, I would soon follow. I gave my horse to a man to hold for me while I went in to the chapple; I found it to be a holy day and surprised to see only a few old people in the church. I performed my prayers, after which mounted my horse and soon after meet the procession which accounted for the few left in the chapple. I made a drawing of the chapple which is called Cap Saunta Chapple. It stand on the right hand of the road going to Quebeck, off from the road.

A league from this we crossed a ferry, the most quick and the most dear, and two leagues further we stop'd to feed and refresh, but could get nothing but a dish of milk. The woman of the house is a shoemaker and was at work when we entered her house. After we left this we stop'd at two post houses, but could not obtain anything to eat either for ourselves or horses. They recommended us to go on some small distance further where lived a rich French farmer, who would no doubt give us entertainment for the night, a Monsieur Bassett. We arrived at the house and with all the French I was master off I prevailed on the family to let us stay here all night. After some time, Mosieur Bassett came in from the field with some more of his household and gave us a welcome, oats and hay for the horses. The family appeared to be well pleased by our being there. At supper two very large earthen dishes where served up. About twelve of us sat round the table, each with a spoon dipping in rotation with uniformity like soldiers at a mess. By this time I had learned to carry my own sclasp knife.

Wednesday morning 6 oclock, set off and crossed a ferry. We pass'd a structure, a kind of canopy, elevated, the top supported by four pillows [*pillars*] with a partition grate halfway up between each pillow, and in the centre of the structure the image of our Saviour carved, as large as a man, naild to a cross, and painted. We crossed over some steep mountains and got within two leagues of Quebeck. We stop'd at an inn on the right hand of the road keep by Mr. Eveland, a German. In the meanwhile we breakfasted and dress'd ourselves. Mr. Eveland went to Quebeck to procure a stable and a lodging for us. Mrs. Eveland, a French lady, churned fresh butter while the coffee was making.

We arrived into Quebeck at 2 o'clock and put up in the suburbs near St. Johns Gate at one Shenegrave, a Frenchman. Next morning Ricketts arrived from Montreal. We build our circus at the S. W. of the town within the walls of Quebeck. We performed two months to good business; I had about 3 hundred dollars for my benefit. The British artilary officers gave me permission to have the assistance of some of their engeneers in making fireworks for me, who also presented me with some very valueable receipt in the nature of fireworks with a correct explenation of the compositions. I was introduced in to their laboratory and armory, which was a great treat to me.

General Brescot [*Prescott*] was the governor at this

time. His daughter, married to an officer, died while we where here. The merchants of Quebeck launched the largest vesel they ever had on the stocks. She struck her stern in the mud and broke in the waist, so obliged to sell her for what she would bring.

Here I meet Mr. Moore, formerly an actor with Mr. Allen in Philad'a, now the King's Printer, and Mr. Bentley, who was the leader of the band to Allen, in a high office too.

The faint remains of the American camp and intrenchments of [17]76 is yet visible on the Plains of Abraham.

This town is well secured by a strong high wall with broad ramparts all round the town, with guard houses over the town gates, deep and wide ditches on the outside. From the upper town you can look in to the chimney toops of lower town. Lower town is situated on the water side where the sailors all keep. It is something like the Point at Baltimore. The govenor's Castle is a fine building and makes a handsome appearance, with his lifeguard of grenediers. A statue of Gen'l Wolf is placed at the corner of a street. The narrow passage and lofty rock where Montgomery was kill'd has a strange appeerence.

I visited an Indian village called Lorette to get an Indian for Mr. Ricketts to stand on his shoulders between two horses. The Indian I got told me by pointing to the sun that he would be in Quebeck the next day when the sun stood just in the same place, which he accordingly did. He came with 6 more Indians.

After performing two months in Quebeck, we returnd to Montreal. In our journey we stop'd again at the coopers house who lives near the bridge at the River Delue. It was a luckey circumstance that we did not cross the bridge, for we had scarsly been a half an hour in the house, when the post rider in a chaise, going full trot over the bridge, when he arrived in the center the whole bridge broke down. He and his horse where dash'd between rocks and kill'd. He was the master of the post house living at Masgeuronge.

We stop'd and performed two weeks at Montreal on our return. I had a nother middling good benefit. And now we prepared to return to the United States again. On the last night's performance the roof of the circus was crowded and would not be drove off. Hutchins the groom fired a gun loaded with peas among them and put out an eye of a young man. The master suet Ricketts, and made him pay eight hundred dollars damage. Hutchins was obliged to hide himself, else the mob would have kill'd him. He got a guide to conducd him over the lines to a house on the lake, and there wait till we call'd for him. This affair detained us some days and attended a good deel of trouble to Mr. Ricketts.

I now bid adue to Canada, a fine country and I am much delighted with it. Travellers have always visited Canada with rapture. A fine fertile country, rich and happy, affords a thousand scenes for amusement. The fancy can scarcely imagine a more delightfull region. The noble River St. Lawrence, pasing through a champain teritory, is

adorned on each side with one continued chain of settlements or rather one village for nearly four hundred miles.
The city of Quebec and Montreal—the parish churches,
parish houses—and more compact clusters near them—fur-
nishes a great variety of edifices worthy the attention of
strangers. The city of Quebeck by nature and art is one of
the strongest fortifications possessed by the British nation.
From the citadal and upertown the eye is entertained in
every direction with pleasing landscapes. South west, Point
Levis and the extensive well settled country in the rear, the
view is bounded by the horizon as far as the eye can reach;
north the River St. Charles, the distant Indian village of
Lorette, and the gentle slope of the small hills variegated
with spires of churches and neat formed houses entertain
you with a large display of beautifull objects for the pencil
of the limner. Within a mile the benevolent heart is
charmed with a sight of that noble charity, the General
Hospital, a place for the sick and poor, supported, en-
dowed, and attended by pious venerable females, an
institution exceeded by few in its noble acts of humanity.
The hospitals of Quebec, Montreal, and Philadelphia may
challenge the world for needness and regularity.

West from the fortification you see the extensive Plains
of Abrams where Wolf and Montcalm fell, where Wooster,
Montgomery, and an hardy valiant corps of Americans
endured the hardship of a winter's campaign in 1776. East
the isle of Orleans and the water scene exhibited by the
confluence of the River St. Charles and St. Lawrence are

not less interesting than the others. The falls of Mountmorency, the Cove where Wolf landed, the place where Wolf
and Montgomory fell, are parts of the many places which
travellers of every grade visets with a variety of pleasing
reflections.

On the 20th of October, we set off, crossed the ferry of
St. Lawrence to La Prairie, from thence to St. Johns,
entered our names in the guard house, had stalls build on
board of a schooner for our horses to sail on the Lake
Champlain from this to Skeensborough. After we where
under way we pass'd the last British garison. In the
afternoon we saw a white flag on the beach before a tavern
keep by one Rouse; we suspected it to be Hutchins, our
groom's signal. The captain sent his boat to shore for him.
The British deserters generally come to this house, being
within the American line, and sometimes perish in the
wilderness from cold and hunger, and very often taken, as
the British employ savages to be on the look out.

In the evening we arrived off Cumberlandhead, and
obliged to come too to render an account to the custom
house. We came too and anchored near the shore and
[decided] to make this our nights harbour. It happened that
the gentleman who keeps the customhouse was at Plattsbourgh when we pass'd thro' there, and expressed a pleasure to see us again. He politely invited us to stay all night
at his house. The son made a collection of the neighbours
of ladies and gentlemen and we had a kind of a ball and

singing. Next day we where over taken by a tremendous storm in a place where the Lake Champlain makes 20 mile a cross. One of our horses fell and got partley under one of the other horses, and with dificulty we got him up again and lashed him up. Every night we made a harbour. We arrived safe at last at Skeenborough (alias Whitehall).

NAMES OF THE TOWNS I PASSED THRO' AND SOME
I VISITED WHILE IN CANADA

La Torti [*La Tortue*]
La Prairie [*Laprairie*]
St. Johns [*St. Jean*]
Montreal
San Suplee [*San Sulpice*]
La Valterry [*Lavaltrie*]
St. Charles
St. Antwin [*St. Antoine*]
Batist Grand [*Batiscan*]
St. Polee [*St. Paulin*]
St. Ann [*Ste. Anne de la Pérade*]
Grondeen [*Les Grondines*]
La Sheene [*Lachine*]
Long gale [*Longueuil*]
Saint Louis
Point Clara [*Pointe Claire*]
Busherwheel [*Boucherville*]

Barkee
Ottowa River
Lildupah [*Isle du Pads*]
River de lue [*Rivière du Loup*]
Monshis [*Yamachiche*]
Point da Lack [*Pointe du Lac*]
Three Rivers [*Trois Rivières*]
Maskinosha [*Maskinonge*]
River da Collet [*Rivière Nicolet*]
Cap de la Madlin [*Cap de la Madeleine*]
Du Chambo [*Deschambault*]
St. Loubinare [*Lotbinière*]
Cap. Sauntay [*Cap Santé*]

Under Shamble mountain [*Chambly Mt.*]

Point of Traumble [*Pointe aux Trembles*]

Ville de Varene [*Varennes*]

Harponga [?]

Vashare [*Verchères*]

Baconcure [*Bécancour*]

William Henry or Sorrel [*Sorel*]

St. Croix

St. August [*St. Augustin*]

St. Nicolas

Cap de Rouge [*Cap Rouge*]

Coaghnawago [*Caughnawaga*]

La Twa Rivier [*Trois Rivières*]

Lorette [*L'Ancienne Lorette*]

From Skeenborough, we proceeded on our journey by land. September 1st we arrived at Lansingbourgh and [performed] a few night to good house. 6 miles from Lansingbourgh stands the town of Troy. We build a day circus, but got so little success that we bid it good bye after the 2d night. We return'd for two days more to Lansingbourgh and then set off and arrived at Albany. We put up at the best inn. I advised Mr. Ricketts to give an entertainment in the ball room of this inn for one night only. The bill was recitations, songs, dances, and ground and lofty tumbling. We succeeded and cleared one hundred dollars; it was done more out of a frolic than the want of money, for I was surprized when Mr. Ricketts consented to it. I never heard him speak or sing previous to this before an audience; he sung "The High Mettlet Racer" with judgment, and I think I may lay claim to be the first that ever sung "The Dutch Fisherman" in America—November 1798.

We crossed the ferry over the Hutson River in to New York state, and travellet by land to New York. In this rout I saw the large tree where André was taken.[11] We entered [New] York through Harlem. We made a stop at New York and performed two weeks after which we proceeded on to Philadelphia. The cold weather was approaching.

We all set to work to get the circus in a fit stile to open for the winter. I finished my house in South Street and settled my family in it and made everything as comfortable as possible.

PART THREE

[With the Chestnut Street Theatre]

W E OPENED THE NEW circus in Chesnut Street with the following company; the New Theatre play'd 3 times a week and we 3 time a week.

NAMES OF RICKETTS' COMPANY

Mr. John B. Ricketts and F. Ricketts, Jno. Durang, Mr. Rowson, Mrs. Rowson, Miss Curry [Correy], Master Hutchins, and a Mrs. Decker.

All the labour of the ring and stage rested on me. I was the clown in the ring, the Harlequin on the stage. All the pantomimes and ballets got up and under my direction, I made all the fireworks, rode the Tailor, the hunter over bars, jumpt through a sun a horseback, drunken peasant with the change in a bag on two horses, still vaulting, carried Ricketts on my shoulders, in the group of *The Pyramids of Egypt* (the top figure), slack rope and wire, songs and dances.

This winter through the carlessness of a drunken carpenter who was in the employ of the circus, who let a candle stand under the roof of a room above the stable where he keep his bottle, set fire to the back part of the circus while yet the horsemanship was going on. *Don Juan* was to have been the stage entertainment of the night. I had just rode the Tailor and dressing for *Don Juan* when the fire was discovered. We had the good fortune to save all the horses, the scenery and wardrobe and every moveable article, even the doors, windows, and pillows of the front [ispiece]. The circus was entirely burnt to the ground to the great loss of Mr. Ricketts and company, and deprived me of a benefit.

At this time we where all at a stand what to do. I soon resolved on a plan to provide for the company; Mr. Ricketts lent his scenery and wardrobe. I took the company to Lancaster [1] and fitted up a theatre, arranged the business for them. I stopt and performed two nights with them. Governor McKean [2] patronised us. I saw them in a fair way to go on and told them it rested on their own conduct to succeed, and left them and went home to live with my family.

While I was absent, which must have been known by some of my dishonest neighbours, they stole about a coard of wood out of my yard, not withstanding I had a trusty dog to guard the yard, who I suspect was well known to them and easily baited. I had not been home two weeks when Mr. Rowson wrote to Ricketts to help them back to Philad'a, which he did to save his scenery and wardrobe. I then rented the old theatre in South Street at 20 dollars a night and opened it with Ricketts company and a few others whom I engaged. [3] Tho' the business was very poor, yet I went on and got them all a subsistance. At my own benefit I flew from the gallary to the back part of the stage thro' a bust [*burst*] of firework; I got 3 hundred dollars by it. After this, or by this time, Mr. Ricketts had disposed of the wreck of his circus and reconciled, resumed the management and engagement of his company again, and went on to Baltimore, to open a circus build by subscription, for Mr. Franklin who did not succeed in performing long. The circus stood in a back street near the falls and middle bridge. I took boarding with Mr. Jones, a shoemaker, at the bottom of the marsh market for my whole family and keep my horse at Mrs. Gisler's stable. We had very good business. End of the season I had three hundred dollars at my benefit. Mr. Ricketts discharged all his company except those who where of use in horsmanship. From this we moved on to Anapolis, and from this to try the fortune of a cercumference tour.

Going by land with the horses from Philadelphia to Baltimore, we passed through Weeds Ferry (miles) 4; Plough 7; Chester 4; Practical Farmer 7; Wilmington 8; Newport 3; Tanton 2; Christiana 9; Dram Shop 7; Elk [*Elkton*] 3; Robinson' Crusoes Hut 3; Charleston 7; Susquahanna [*river*] 6; crossing the ferry to Havre de Grace—1⅔; Tavern 5; the Widow Bush 5; Websters 12; Bucks 4; Baltimore 9: total 109 miles.

While we where at Anapolis I hired appartments in the govenor's house and boarded with the steward who had charge of the house during the governor's absence from

town. The circus was built in a field opposide to the
governor's. We got but a poor sort of business and stop'd
here only two weeks; we sold the circus for half price. Our
next destination was for the eastern shores of Maryland. We
crossed the bay of the Chesapeake in a convenient sloop 12
miles to Kenterhook ferry on the Eastern Shores. On this
passage we passed 3 rocks called the Three Sisters. We
landed up in the St. Micheal River; we stoped at this ferry
house one night. Next morning I obtained a carriage to
take on my family to East town [*Easton*], Talbut County.
In the middle of the day, we made a long rest from the
great heat of the sun. We arrived soon in the evening at
Easton and took lodgings at a widow lady's who gave us
plenty of pone bread ⁴ which I never could eat. (We
performed here two weeks and a half.) Coming to Eastown
up the Eastern Bay from Kenterhook Ferry, which is keep
by Snack, we stop'd at Queen Anns town and could get
nothing to eat, pass'd by a place called Hole in the Wall.
From Easton we went on to Cambridge in Dorcester County.
We cross'd a ferry two miles wide and took lodgings with
the captain of the ferry boats who lives near the river. And
our circus was build opposide to our lodgings. To paint
this circus I made a substitute with charcoal and hard red
chalk I found on the banks here. The gentlemen of
Cambridge made up a party for a dinner to partake in a
pleasend spot on a green shaded by a wood. As Mr.
Ricketts, myself, and our band of music (Mr. Brookes was
the leader) we where politely invited, Mr. Ricketts took on

his part to form and decorate an arbour under which the rustic dinner table and seats where placed with a well provided dinner and liquor of all discriptions. I took on myself the construction of a display of fireworks for the evening in front of the arbour. Every gentleman of the party had some work allotted towards the entertainment. In the evening every gentleman who had some skill in music joined the band, songs and toast where mingled with the sparkling glass in harmony and pleasure of the citizens.

We meet with as much success as the small place would afford, for one week and a half, when we sold the circus as usuel for half price. (We returned.) Captain Fowler took us a cross the ferry (the ferry is over Chopank River). We arrived to dinner at Mr. Newman's in Eastown, and immediately proceeded on our journey to Centre Ville in Queen Anns county, beautyfull roads all the way. We pass'd a place on this road called Church Hill. We met with great success in this small town for ten days. From this we went on to East Chestertown; we cross'd a ferry 3 quarters of a mile wide crossing a river runing by Chester in Kent County (Chester River).

We performed here with good success for two weeks, when we closed and returned to Anapolis by way of Kenderhook Ferry; this was in August 1799. We lodged one night in Anapolis; next morning, 4 miles off, cross'd a ferry and arrived in the evening at Bladensbourg, stop'd their all night and breakfast. We continued our journey and passed through Washinton City the same day and put up in Georgetown joining the city. We procured a large tobacco wharehouse from a Mr. Templeman, who did everything in his power to assist, accomodate, and patronise us. He is a very rich man, a tall well handsome made, and I have strong believe that this [was] the very same Mr. Templeman, who was the celebrated wire dancer who made a fortune in the old Theatre South Street, Philad'a, formerly.

I put up at first at the head inn at 2 dollars a piece for boarding. I after got into a private family who had broke up [their] grocery store, where you could not sleep for the rats, who where at high sport all the night, knawing and playing with the remnets of what was left in the store, and who would visit our bed room through the doors they knawed for themself to enter. In this neighbour hood I met with Mr. Travers, a sociable gentleman in the business of a store, who formerly lived in High Street, Baltimore, and my neighbour on my first visit there. I mention him on account of the great politeness he allways paid me.

We performed two weeks in Georgetown to a numorous and genteel audiance. From this we proceeded on to Alexandria, 8 miles from Georgetown. We crossed the ferry at G.town, about a mile wide. We erected a circus in Alexandria; I took boarding at a German family. The Virginia Company where performing in the theatre at the time. I was in to Mr. Robins' benefit; he had a poor house. We advertised our performance for three successive days to perform, and no one came near the place. Mr. Ricketts gave the place his blessing, left the circus stand for a monument of poverty, and we all mounted our horses, and off in full speed without saying good bye. Alexandria is a handsome town laid out and resemble Philadelphia more then any other town in America and lays on the Patomic River.

We got to Georgetown on the same evening and performed three days more there to good business. From this we returned to Anapolis and made an attempt to perform in the forenoon but nobody came. We where advertised to perform in conjunton with a Frenchman who had made a grand display of fireworks to take place on the same evening of the day we attempted to perform in Anapolis (in our circus at Baltimore). At 11 o'clock in the morning we saw no prospect to perform in Anapolis. We where at this time ready dressed in our performing clothes; we put on our street clothes over our performing clothes, mounted our horses and hurry'd on to Baltimore with all possible speed and arrived at the circus in Baltimore a little after dark. We found the place all alive; the French gentleman was going on with his firework to a full house. By the time he was done, we where ready and concluded the evening's entertainment with horsemanship (smart work). We made but a short stay in Baltimore. When we returned to Philad'a Mr. Ricketts had no choice left but to hire the ruins of that once elegant circus build by Monsieur Lelson [*Lailson*], which [had] proved his ruin. His company was too numerous and the expense of the building too great. He

brought in to this country many and of first rate performers, the most splendid wardrobe and brilliand trappings
for the ring and stage. He would ride in equestrian
procession with his full company magnificently dress'd,
mounted on elegant horses (male and female) through the
street of Philad'a on the play afternoon to intice the public.
In the winter a heavy snow lay on the dome, which was the
hemispherical arch covering the ring; it fell in on a
Sunday. No one was hurt, but it put an end to Mr. Lelson's
performance and company. He went from Philad'a and I
have never heard since what has become of him.

The circus stood the corner of Prune and Fifth Street.
Mr. Ricketts occupy'd the front dwelling part and the
stables for his horses, which where all in good order. The
circus was got in the best order it could be in its situation
without a roofe over the ring. The audience part was still
covered, but the lights in the night made a dim reflection
which caused the performance to go off gloomy. We
worry'd on for a few weeks; at lenth Mr. Ricketts began to
get out of heart with doing business in this bodge way. His
mind wandering unreconciled, he resolved to leave America. Accordingly he made his arrangement for departure.
His entreaty could not persuade me to go with him; I was
settled in a home with my family and would not leave that
to seek a living in a foreign country and trust to chance,
while I was a citizen of a town with the best market in the
world. It became necessary to stay at home and take care of
a growing family.

Mr. Ricketts chartered a small vessel, constructed stalls on deck and each horse secured in slings, laid in hay and oats, and took lumber enough to build a circus. He set off from Philad'a with himself and brother, the groom and a stable boy, Master Hutchins, and a Mr. Miller for his carpenter, the same carpenter who sat fire to his circus. Mr. Ricketts waited two days at Newcastle for Mr. Mat Sully who had agreed to go with him, but disappointed him. Ricketts on way to the West Indias was taken by a French privateer and taken into Gautaloup and there all his effects, horses, and lumber where sold at public vendue for the prize money. By good luck and management of Mr. Hutchins, the groom, who saved Mr. Ricketts' favorite silver mounted broadsword and pistols by hideing them beneeth the horses manure, howe'r, some merchant of Gaudoloup bought all the horses and lumber in for Ricketts. He errected his circus and in a few nights paid all off and once more stood on his own firm.

After that he visited some of the other islands. In the meantime Master Hutchins and the carpenter died. F. Ricketts married and was about to leave the island and his wife, when the governor put him in the cells; he got out again, and came to America again. Mr. J. Ricketts sold all his horses to great advantage and had made an immense of money; he chartered an old vessel to take him to England; the vessel foundered and he was lost with all his money at sea.

I heard of F. Ricketts being in Boston. I wrote to him

and to come on to Philad'a and administer to his brother's property, which was the three lots the circus stood on in Chesnut Street. He came company of a dashing knowing Yankey who persuaded him from my good adwise, and sold the whole property for eighteen hundred dollars. When F. Ricketts and the Yankey waited on me, the Yankey had already laid on a good sum for a gold watch and new clothes. I told F. Ricketts to leave the money in the hands of good freeholders and draw as occasion may require; that he would not listen too, but he set off with the money and the Yankey towards Boston. And in a few weeks he return'd and told me the Yankey got all the money from him, and then send him away. F. Ricketts joint a circus party and performed on the open commons at Mr. Laudenslagers in Baltimore. The last I heard of him, he had been enlisted in the servince of the United States laying in camp at Yorktown when I was there, and marched off for the Lakes.

At this time I was bequeath'd to ruminate for myself some new employment. I purchased an elegant bay horse from Mr. Hughs who had him trained for the race course. He was a good quarter horse; I paid one hundred dollars for him. I gave this horse the name Cornplanter, as he resembled Mr. Ricketts' charger Cornplanter. I broke this horse into the circus exercise in a few weeks in my own yard. I made a compleat charger of him; he would go on his knees or lay down, leap over the bars, run after the

Tailor, and a handsome saddle horse for the street, and work in harness.

I engaged Lelson's circus for a short time and made up a small company. Mr. Degraft, a man who taught riding and well skill'd in horses, joined me. He procured 3 horses more. We went on in some tolarable good order in the ring with some stage performance. One night as I was riding Cornplanter in a suit of armour with a visor on my face and in full speed with a shower of fireworks on the top of my helmet ending with an explosion, the explosion frightened the horse. He jump'd over three benches of the pit, tore a way a patition with his hind legs and landed in the passage of the stable door, and flung me over the orchestra on the stage without any hurt to myself or horse. I found that I did not get paid for my trouble in this scheme. I brought it to a close, and amused myself at home and in my garden. And in the meantime build an addition to my front house, a stable and carriage house at the end of my lot fronting on Small Street and paved both the fronts of South Street and Small Street.

Messrs. Wignell and Reinagle was at this time the managers of the New Theatre in Chesnut Street opposide the statehouse. I applied to Mr. Wignell for an engagement, as he had allways been a good friend to me in the Old American Company. I thought myself sure of an engagement, but to my disappointment [he] told me he could not give me one. I went away meditating whether it could be from prejudice that I did him an injury by performing with Ricketts, or some particular cause. I waited on him again and ask'd him if he had any objection agains'd my personel character or any other motive; he told me, in his usuel gentlemany manner, that he could not afford to give me the salary which I had been accustomed to receive lately of Mr. Ricketts. I told him as that was done away with, I should agree to conform with the limits and rules of his arrangement, be what it would. [In] that case he told me he will be happy to give me an engagement; he frankly made me an offer which I excepted and immediately became a member of the Philadelphia company with the determination not to quit it to join any other theatre. I rely'd on my own conduct to make it a parmanency. I have succeeded in my resolution in years of succession and speak with pride of this company. Its regulations are founded on good principle and respectebility, first established by Mr. Wignell, a worthy gentleman and man of honour. He gained nothing by the institution, but all the labour and anxiety rested on him. Mr. Reinagle shared with him the burden of the debts.

Mr. Wignell had brought out the plan of the new theater from London compleatly build in miniuture, a true model of the new theatre, to gether with the front drop, an extensive and brilliant wardrobe and music. In 1793 Mr. Wignell brought over to America from England a numerous full company of actors, some of great talent. On their arrival in the Deleware in consiquence of the yellow fevre raging in Philadelphia, they where obliged to ride quarrentine, and landed on the New Jersey shores till it was safe to venture into the city.

THE NAMES OF THE PERFORMERS WHO COMPOSED THE COMPANY.[5]

Messrs. Wignell and Reinagle, Managers
Mr. Wignell for the Stage Department
and Mr. Reinagle of the Music

Mr. Warren the American—Falstaff and Benevolent Merchant

Mr. Moreton — Genteel first line

Mr. Chalmers — Genteel sprightly line

Mr. Witlock — Genteel steady old gentlemen

Mr. Francis — Sprightly old men, Tag, and [. . .]

Mr. Green — Abelino

Mr. Marshal — Lovers &c.

Mr. Darly (great singer) — Hecate and High Priest

Mr. Blissett — Doctor Caious, Sheepface, Jerry Sneck

Mr. Bernard — Shackaback

Mr. Fennel — King Lear

Mr. Cross

Mr. Darley, Jun. — in song and choruses

Mr. Warrel, Sen.

two Messrs. Warrell, Jun. — in the ballets

Mr. L. Estrange — Prompter and actor

Mr. Milbourn — Painter and actor; ground Harlequin
Mr. Holland — Principle scene painter
Signieor Doctor — Tumbling &c.
Mr. Byrn — Ballett master and great dancer
Mr. Hardinge
Mr. Gillingham — Leader of the orchestra, band of 20
Mr. Bates

Ladies

Mrs. Merry — the chaset Julianer
Mrs. Witlock
Mrs. Shaw
Mrs. Warrel
Mrs. Oldmixon — the Lucretia Martal
Mrs. Byrn — Irish Lilt dance
Mrs. Francis — the Mrs. Malaprop and Mrs. Quickly
Mrs. Doctor — Mrs. Warren — Mrs. Gillingham
Miss Arnold — Miss Delenge — Miss Milbourne
Mrs. Bernard — Mrs. Hardinge — Mrs. Marshal
Miss L. Strange
(Mr. Strickland, master carpenter; Mr. Flour, machinist,
Gibbons, the master tailor, Mr. Wood, treasurer)

A list of performers who have since joined the Company [6]

Mr. Cooper — the generalissimo tragedian — Mr. Twaits
— Mr. McKenzie — Mr. Cone — Mr. Fulenton — Mr.
Cain — Mr. Robins — Mr. Bray — Mr. Duff — Mr.

Jefferson — Durang, Sen. — C. Durang — F. Durang —
Harris — Scrivenor — Taylor — Usher — Saymour —
McKenney — Burk — Abbercrombie — Prigmore — Mc-
Farland — Jones — Hathwell — Willes — King — Car-
ter — Bailey — Mr.   Barrett — Wallack — Hughes —
Martin — Goodwin — Jones — Jackson — Anderson —
Jacobs — T. Jefferson — Herbert — Stuard — Savage —
Robison — Drummond — Wilmot — Hopkins — Shar-
nock — Mestayer — Briars — Allen — Miller — Downie
— Waring — Leg — Thompson — Emberton — Horton
— Lewis — Green — Weedley — Morris — Johnson —
Lopez — Loaf — Morgan — Seerson — Doyel — Sanders
— Mrs. Seymour — Mrs. Melmouth — Mrs. Bray — Mrs.
Harris — Mrs. Solomon and daughter — Mrs. Jones —
Mrs. Barrett — Mrs. Carter — Blissett's good wife — Miss
Mullen — Mrs. Jackson — Miss C. and K. Durang —
Mrs. Wallack — Miss Seymour — Miss Hathw[. . .]
— Mrs. Darley — Mrs. Jefferson — Mrs. Anderson —
Mrs. Jacobs — Miss Pettit — Mrs. Simson — Mrs. Placide
— Miss White — Mrs. Savage — Mrs. Mestayers — Mrs.
Allen — Mrs. Downie — Miss   Abbercrombie — Miss
Prigmore — Mrs. Waring — Mrs. Leg — Mrs. Cloud —
Mrs. McFarland — Mrs. Morris — Mrs. Gillasbie and
daughter — Mr. Entwizle — Mrs. Entwizle — Galbreath
— Sir John Oldmixon — Mr. Woodham — Mrs. Wood-
ham — Mr. Fox — Mr. Rutherford — Master Cuningham
— Thos. Turney — Webster — Lucas — Harwood

In the first winter of my engagement in the new theatre Chesnut Street, I assisted Mr. Francis in his dancing academie at Harmony Hall in teaching his pupils in the art of dancing. Mr. Francis told me he would give me a suit of clothes for my labour at the close of the school. He gave me a check on the bank for one hundred dollars, and on the following winter Mr. Francis took me in pardnership and devided the profits of the school and ball equelly with me for the time of twelve or fourteen years in succession in the greatest amity and harmony. I shall allways hold and offer my highest esteem and respect for Mr. Francis, not only for his gentlemany politeness to me, but for his own private character. He is the cheerfull generous benevolant man; his friends are allways happy in his company.

I must remark that Mr. Francis and Mr. Ricketts and myself are particularly of very hasty temper and that for the many years I have been concearned in business with both those gentlemen, we never exchanged one word in anger. Their disposition is like my own, soon hot and soon cold, not to offer an insult, and the first ready to make apology if in the fault, and ready to serve them with a good heart.

At the close of the season, Mr. Wignell advancet my salary and the company moved on to Baltimore. I went with them for the first time. At the end of a short season I returned to Philad'a to my family. I was not long at home when Mr. Broomly, a New England man, called on me in great style and offered me an engagement at 30 dollars a week to go with him and perform in Lancaster. He had engaged a great wire dancer at 30 dollars a week. I went with him to Lancaster. Mr. Manager Broomly could do nothing himself; his dependance rested intirely on this wire dancer and myself. I sat to work and painted a paper scene, wings, and frontispiece, and decorated a small stage. In the meantime this great wire dancer lay in bead all day, and the manager was losing tickets at playing cards in a room below.

We went on performing to full houses. Every night I found the principle labour fell on me, and this wire dancer, tho' he was very great on the wire, he did not please much. His manners where uncouth, without address, manners, or respect towards the audience. And thro' laziness he began to counterfeit lameness. On a night when the house was very full, I was obliged to perform on the wire, instead of him. I made an apology and excepted and gave general satisfaction on the wire, so the whole night's performance was done by myself. I got two weeks salary from Mr. Broomly, and then brought the whole matter to a close. I performed two nights on my own account and then returned home where I remained till I joined the new theatre in Baltimore for a short season and then returned to Philad'a for the winter season.

Mr. Wood at the end of this season in Baltimore went to England. Mr. Wells became treasurer. Mr. Wells was suceeded in that employment by Mr. Evans; he continued in the office a few years and laid up some money.

Mr. Evans before he step'd in to the treasury department was the property[man] of the theatre and his wife the house keeper. The present propertyman is Mr. Ward, a man whom I respect with my highest esteem. His worthyness commands the love and respects of the managers and all who know him for a religious, honest, innofensive benevolant domestic man. Mrs. Savelle is the house keeper of the theatre, and industrious, carefull woman, well calculated for the situation. Mrs. Gray is the mistress of the ladies' wardrobe, a worthy genteel lady. Mrs. Crosbye is the assistant in the wardrobe, a very genteel worthy Lady. Mr. McCubbin was the master tailor in the gentleman's wardrobe for several years; he was a genteel behaved man. Mr. Harbaugh is the present master tailor, a worthy and trusty man, very capaple for the situation and respected by all who know him. Mr. Strickland was the master carpenter, a good natured worthy man. Mr. Commings is the present master carpenter, a worthy industrious and ingenious man whom I respect. He has a friendly heart, in fact, all the carpenters engaged in the theatre are worthy respectable men and their private character and public conduct has allways been genteel and polite, reserved in language and manners. I wish I could say so much for the actors in general.

Messrs. Robins and Holland where the master painters; Messrs. Warren and Reinagle are the present head painters. Those are all gentlemany men who execute their work in a masterly manner to the great satisfaction of the public.

At the close of the theatre the company opened the Baltimore theatre for two months in the beginning of the
summer till the 10th of June, and after that they pass'd the
summer in Washington and Alexander. I never went with
them to Washington as I calculated it never would pay the
expense of myself and family. I returned home on my
horse to Philadelphia, 181[ ]. I purchased a frame house
of 20 foot square standing on a lot joining the lot I live on
from Sam'l Rickey. I pay'd him half of the money down. I
painted a set of scenery and drapary for a small stage of
theatrical performance, and formed a company composed
of my own family, with my brother, and we set out for
Lancaster and performed at Mr. Rohrer's ball room with
great success.

From Lancaster I took my small company on to Harrisburg. I converted the store house of Colonel Brook near the
ferry into a theatre. I constructed boxes and galery; my
stage was compleatly theatrical, 12 foot front and fifteen
deep, five wings of a side, with stage doors, frontispiece,
and green curtain. We had crowded houses every night at
50 cents for the box and 25 for the galary and very little
expense. I boarded with Mr. Snider at the ferry house, very
obliging people. I sent my son Charles (at the age of ten
years) to Philad'a on a business which he executed with
correctness according to my instructions. I tied some
money round his waiste underneath of his shirt and bid
him not to pull off his trowsers going to bed. I sent him off
in the stage to Lancaster where he lodged one night, and set

down his name for the return of [the] stage next day. He
went on in the stage to Philad'a and there set down his
name to return in the stage. He waited on Mr. Rickey and
paid him the last half of the money I owed him on the
purchase of the house. He then purchased for me some
books and other articles I was in want off. Lodged one night
at his grandmother's, who lived in my house; next morning
he set off for Lancaster and Harrisburg, bringing with him
his brother Ferdinand. When he arrived at our lodging Mr.
Snider expressed surprize and told me that he could not
trust his son of 16 to do a particular errent to the other end
of the town.

The night after I closed the theatre, I gave a small
exhibition of firework on the Susquehana River opposide
to Harrisburg. I took my firework and music in a large
ferry boat and anchored a short distance from the shore.
Next morning I set off with my company to Lebenon and
erected a theatre in the unfinish'd third story of Esquire
Steover's house, a spacious room over the whole house. I
performed here to great success for ten days. Mrs. Steover
told me that I was the only and the first person that her
husband ever allowed or permitted to play the fiddle in the
house. Nor would he have permitted now but from the
strong recommandation I had from some of the first people
and lawyers of Harrisburg.

I set off from this place, leaving the towns people well
gratified with the invitation to visit them again. This part of
the country or neighbourhood is generally inhabited by a
sect of people called Manistes, or Dunkerds.[7] They are

Germans; the aged men wear their beards very long and clothes very plain and generally home spun, of their own manufactoring. I am the only person that ever succeeded in performing among them which was in consequence of my speaking the German language. I spoke the words of the characters I performed in German, and sometimes I would introduce a German song together with dancing, ballette, pantomimes, feats on the rope and wire, transparencies, shipfights &c. I pleased them very much and paid me well for my trouble.

I allways studied the taste and manners of the people before whome I intended to perform, and gain their patronage. My great attraction was to gain the attention of the leading people of the place to visit me and that secured the other classes of people to follow, and assured me success. Accordingly I selected and arranged my bill affair to suit their taste, and I never failed in my object. The whole fabric of my scheme was build on the foundation of my own private conduct, to make myself to be respected by the rich and poor. I observed a reserve of industry and sobriety, a compliant address conformed with the manners and rules of the family I lived with and inhabitants, found no fault, tho' it sometimes was not so good as I had been accustomed too. I pay'd my way, I secured the love and commerce of the people who where allways glad to see me again with a cheering welcome; no man need to risk'd on a country scheme unless he will keep within the strict bounds of my plan.

I hired a country wagon to take on my baggage to the

town of Reading. I rode on before to provide lodgings. The
next day after I had settle my family, two gentlemen
lawyers, Spade and Evens,[8] politely interested themselves
to serve me. Being the leading men of the place their words
prevailed; they obtained for me a large ball room at the
principle inn, sign of Gen'l Washington, keep by Mrs.
Wood, an accomplished genteel lady. I performed two
weeks to great success. I had my bills printed at a
Republican German printer and advertised in the Federal
English paper. From this town I went on to Philad'a by the
way of Norristown.

At the intervals of my employment at the theatre and
dancing academy, I put into operation the extension of my
theatrical summer scheme, and bring it to a regular
symtum [*system*]. I selected and provided myself with a
library of such dramatic plays which I knew would please
best in the country, of tragedys, comedys, farces, and
operas. I curtail'd them, but still preserved as much as
possible the plot and incidents compactly within the com-
pass to be performed by two arrangements, that is by a
company of one lady and three gentlemen, or two ladies
and five gentlemen. I thought that my surety would be in
being prepared for an alternative, to make an additional
arrangement in calculation of depending on myself and
family alone, not to be left in the lurch.

For the caprice of some actors are such as you cannot
calculate on to a certainty; their affability on the commencement of their engagement has the sincere appearance

of reliance, but as soon as they are in possession of money, a consequent dignity will arise and so alter their manner and conduct as to cause the business to be done in a careless lazy way, and take on themselves the assurance to dictate the manager's business and make objections, especially some woman actresses whose ambition soars above their ability, and ever jealous at the praize and applause of a nother actress. The most vain and mischievous artfull woman who assumed the name of actress was Mrs. Blissett!!! a name she has disgraced. An unexperienced manager who takes such actors on his first trial will not be able to take them to one or two towns before a revolt takes place and the whole scheme is knock'd in the head. I know it from experience and would have several times been left in great difficulties, but for my own inventions and ingenious provisional preparations against such storms. And by that means I secured my business to the end of my summer season.

My remarks are not aimed at all actors generally; quite the contrare, for the reputation of the theatres stands on a foundation which is propt by the respectability and well-governed conduct of some of the actors, whose personel qualifications recommends them to mix in the first societies, and respected by all parties, with the exception of a few whose prejudice prevails to speak ill of everybody. An actor's heart is open and free to charity.

About this time Mr. Wignell died and the management devolved on Mrs. Wignell. I was sorry to see her in the situation, harass'd by some of the performers as she was. Mr. Warren relieved her of that anxiety by marriage and took on himself the management, in whose reign the well-meaning actors are happy and perform their duty without the strict observance of the articles which is put up in the Green Room to enforce punctuality to the careless.

I purchased a good family carriage from Mr. Hanes, coach maker of Philad'a, and bought a horse. When the company went on to Baltimore I took my family by the mail road to Baltimore. After the close of the Baltimore season Mr. Layman of the Columbia Garden [9] engaged me at a salary of fifty dollars a week and a clear benefit. We gave a miscellaneous entertainment under the head of "Concert" twice a week. I constructed a stage with a cover and dressing rooms underneath, an orchestra in the front, a curtain with the decorations of scenery; a circus ring was formed between the stage and the boxes, an elevated galery. The garden was illuminated with veriegated lamps thro' the walks and summer houses. I introduced horsmanship in the ring by Mr. Degraf and myself. Mr. Hupfield was the leader of the orchestra. Singing by Mrs. Coffea. For the ballette and pantomime was my brother, Mr. Mestayers, Mr. Roach, Miss Mullin, myself and sons. The garden was full every night. I closed the garden with a good benefit. I performed two summers in this garden. (Mrs. Layman assumed the rein of management so I quit the garden.)

In one of my journeys to Baltimore, I traveled on at the

slow pace on horse back with the part of Richard the Third in my hand most constant, studying the character with a determination to play the part in the German language in some of the German settlements. I had nearly compleated my study when I arrived at Baltimore. I play'd the part of Richard 3d and Petruchio, the greatest part in German, in Hanover; I allways gave the cues in English.

My second excursion in the country I made my company up with (beside my own family) Miss Mullin, Mr. Goodwin, and Mr. Loaft, a musician; he was an English man, and it was with difficulty that I could keep him sober enough to play. At night he had a black suit of clothes and never undress'd himself, but lay in bed all day, so that when he got up he look'd like a wild bird, feathered. He was something in his make like the figure of Easope; he was a good musician.

I opened my summer theatre in Lancaster at Mr. Roarer's ball room.[10] From Lancaster I went to Reading. I stop'd and boarded with my family and company with Mrs. Wood and performed in her ball room. From Reading I took my company to Harrisburg and performed in Major Brook's storehouse. It just happened to be the time of court, which I found to be a most improper time for any kind of amusement as the country people are engaged at court to very late in the evening. And the citizens are engaged to wait on the country people, therefore you loose the chance of both. And at anytime you cannot calculate on the country people, but only the citizens of a town, who will allways have the generosity and spirit to support you when they are disengaged from the bustle of the courts or the fairs or the races; on any of those occasions it is best to avoid.

From Harrisburg I went on to Carlisle for the first time and performed with great success at a corner house (now occupied by Mr. Umrick). The man was a German baker; he sold my tickets at the bar. He told some of my people that I made more money then he did with his baken and tavern together, which must have been a mistake for I allways have and did draw more custom to his bar or any of the landlords where I stop at than they have been used too on any other time. Besides a good large sum I allways have to pay them for the rent, boarding for myself and company, and necessary expences. Which makes it well worth their while and allways sorry when I was leaving their house.

From this I went to Hanover. I took the road by the celebrated York Springs where I stop'd with my family two hours and dined. I arrived in the evening at Hanover and put up at the stage house keept by Mr. Clapsadle, a very obliging family, and performed in his ball room to crowded houses every night.

I went on to Philad'a from this and joined the company for the winter; in the spring to Baltimore. I took the whole apparatus of my theatrical with me to Baltimore where I still made improvements on them and prepared for the following summer. I performed two weeks at the Pantheon

in Baltimore. The Pantheon is at this present time converted to hold public meetings; a debateing society meet
for sometime. The city springs are attach'd in the front.
This is an ornamentel beauty of Baltimore; the water is
celebrious and conducive to health, and situated in the
elegant street and fashionable prominade leading to Howard's Park within the space of Washington's monument to
the monument in Howard's Park erected in honour and
memorial of those brave Baltimore volunteers who bought
the freedom of the city at the price of their blood, and the
tears of their wives and children.

My next summer tour was from Baltimore to Hanover. I
had in company with me my own family, Miss Mullin, who
was put apprentice to me by her own will and her mother's
wish and entreaties. I watched with a father's care over her
and taught her dancing, singing, and in a short time she
became a usefull actress. A Mr. Drummon was with me
who also became a usefull actor. Mr. Thornton was of my
company this season, a sober and well-behaved civil,
industrious young man; became a usefull actor. While I
was in Hanover I ordered a four wheel light wagon to be
build for me which was compleated by the spring following, compleat with hoops, and sent on to Baltimore to me
by Mr. Eckert.

I set out on my fourth summer tour with my own
carriage and two horses for my family, my wagon compleat with a canvas top and two horses for the baggage and
scenery, and I travelled on horseback. I keep'd the horse,

Cornplanter, for that express purpose to accompany the family and baggage wagon, who I would allways send off a day before, over take it on the road, and then ride on before to make the arrangements in the lodgeings for my family and the company. My plan was to have all the pieces I ment to play in the season studied in the first town and got up with as much correctness as possible, for I well knew that the performers would not study after they once was in pocession of money in a nother town, for I have found them so. Therefore I made my arrangements in the commencement and made a selection for seven or eight nights, the bill affair of each night new, after the first town. I allways mentioned the number of nights at the top of my bill; by that means I had the house fill'd every night and could play every night in succession and then off to the next place. And that was the only way to save myself and make anything, tho' the labour was great.

The following is a catalogue of plays, farces, operas, pantomimes, interludes, ballettes, transparencies,[11] and other entertainments consisting of scenery and machinery got up occasionally at different seasons.

PLAYS
Richard 3d [Shakespeare]
Honey Moon [Tobin]
Pizzaro [Kotzebue/Sheridan]
Lovers Vows [Kotzebue/Dunlap]
John Bull [Colman, Jr.]

Point of Honor [Charles Kemble]
Douglas [Home]
George Barnwell [Lillo]
Voice of Nature [Dunlap]
Mountaineers [Colman, Jr.]
She Stoops to Conquer [Goldsmith]
Catharine and Petruchio [Shakespeare/Garrick]
American Heroine [Dunlap]
Stranger [Kotzebue/Dunlap]

OPERAS
Rosina [Mrs. Brooke]
Poor Soldier [O'Keeffe]
No Song, No Supper [Prince Hoare]
Farmer [O'Keeffe]
Highland Reel [O'Keeffe]

ROMANCE BURLETTAS
Forty Thives [anon.]
Blue Beard [Colman, Jr.]
Tom Thumb the Great [Fielding]
Stoffle Rilbps und Annalis [*Stoofel Rilps, or The Seu-Shwan Wedding*]

FARCES
Lady of the Rock [Holcroft]
Sultan [Bickerstaffe]
Day after the Wedding
Lock and Key [Hoare]
Hunter of the Alps [Dimond]

How to Die for Love
Budged of Blunders
Purse, American Tar [*The American Tar or The Press
Gang Defeated*, William Francis.]
Devil to Pay [Dibdin]
Of Age To Morrow [Dibdin]
Weather Cock
Spoild Child [Bickerstaffe]
Fortune's Frolic [John Till Allingham]
Village Lawyer [William McCready]
Toothach [John Bray]
Raising the Wind [Kenney]
Prize, 2.[5],3.8 [Hoare]
Virgin Unmasked [Fielding]
Mayor of Garret [Foote]
Who is the Dupe? [Mrs. Cowley]
Like Master, Like Man [from King's *Lover's Quarrels*]
Miss in her Teens [Fielding]
Midnight Hour [Mrs. Inchbald]
Tale of Mystery [Holcroft]

INTERLUDES OF ONE ACT
Dr. Lasts' Examination [Foote]
Vintner in the Suds [Ward]
Sylvester Daggerwood [Colman, Jr.]
Lectures on Heads [George Alexander Steevens]
Prologues and Epilogues

Recitations
Songs

BALLETTES
Little Red Riding Hood
Auld Robin Gray
Jack in Distress
Two Philosophers
Two Huntsmen
Caladonian Frolic
Old Soldier, or Two Robbers

DANCES
Hornpipes, Highland Flings
Dwarf Dance, Strathpays, Gavots
Allemandes, Waltzes, Blindfold over Eggs
Minuets, Reels
Dancing on the Slack Wire
Tumbling and Vaulting on the Slack Rope
Leaps thro' a Barrel of Fire

PANTOMIMES
Robinson Crusoe
Death of Harlequin
Devil among the Tailors

[TRANSPARENCIES, &C.]
Phantasmagoria
Brilliencies of Perico, Chineese Fire
American Heroes at Tripoli in Transparencies

Sea Engagements
Perry's Victory
Mac Donough Victory
Italian Shades
Les Ombres chinoise

PART FOUR

A Memorandum and Abstract Journal Taken from My Day Book

IN THE YEAR 1804 I performed in the Anapolis theatre; the company consist only of my own family. On my return to Baltimore, I commenced the first season in Columbia Garden keep by Thos. Leahman and performed two summers with good success; my salary was $50 a week and clear benefit.

1804, I united pardnership with Mr. Wm. Francis teaching a dancing school at Harmoney Hall in Philadelphia.

1806, I performed at the Pantheon in Baltimore.

1806, I taught a dancing school in pardnership with Mr. Francis at the Fountain Inn, keep by Briden and a school at Pampilion's Hotel on the Point.

1807, I opened the old theatre in South Street, Philad'a, with a large company, myself manager. On the night of my benefit I flew from the gallery to the back part of the stage; took on this night $300.

1808, performed in Lancaster at Mr. Rohrer's and Baum's, next at Yorktown, next at Hanover, next at Fredericktown, at Mr. Stalling's Hotel. Cash taken in the four towns: one thousend ninety seven dollars, 95 cents; the whole expense six hundred and eleven dollars, 29 ct. Clear four hundred eighty six dollars, 66 ct.

[18]09, performed at Mr. Stalling's in Fredericktown 13 nights,

Cash taken$289.95 ct.

July 16, I performed at the coffee house in Hagerstown keep by Mr. Smith.

Taken in nine nights$390.51 ct.

Total Expense$220.29 ct.

In July, performed at Col. Snyder's in Chambersburg.

Cash taken in ten nights$382.64 ct.

Expense$187.75 ct.

August 22nd, performed at Mr. Humrick's in Carlisle; every night full houses.

Cash taken in about two weeks$400.00 ct.

The expences$127.57 ct.

Sept. 9, I performed at Mr. Rohrer's, Sign of the King of Prussia, in Lancaster.

Cash taken in 9 nights$286.36 ct.

Expense$ 71.75 ct.

Sept. 22nd, I performed at Peter Eckert's, Sign of the Indian King, in Hanover.

Cash taken in 6 nights at 25 cents a ticket$ 98.61 ct.

Expense of the theatre$ 12.00 ct.

Deposided money with Mr. Eckert to have my wagon

build and left all my theatrical apparatus in his charge till the following season.

1810, June 18th, I opened the season in Lancaster at Mr. Rohrer's; in company, Messrs. Cross, Miller, Miss Mullin.

July 23, performed at Mr. Humrick's in Carlisle.

August 4, performed in Chamberburg at Col. Snyder's to full houses every night. The performers got all good benefits.

August 21, performed at Mr. Fechtig's coffeehouse in Hagerstown, full houses every night.

September, I performed in Fredericktown, at the usuel house, but now keep by Jacob Miller.

October 1st, performed at Hanover, and finished the season here.

1811, June 18, I opened the season in Lancaster at Mr. Whiteside's, Sign of the Fountain, with the company of Mr. and Mrs. Seymour, Mr. Charnock, Mr. Davis, Charles and Ferdinand and Augustus Durang, Mrs. Allport, Mrs. Jefferie, myself and family.

August 7, performed in Yorktown at Peter Wilt's.

[August] 14, performed in Hanover at Peter Eckert's. On leaving this town for Fredericktown we met with an accident. About a mile out of town we had to cross a large brook wherein my horses had been usually watered. When they got into this brook their bridles were loosened to let them drink. On attempting to go on, the leader of a three horse teem could not be managed, but turned round to make for the stable. They pull'd the wagon twice round in this brook and at last upset the wagon, wrench'd one wheel, and about one third of my baggage got wet, so that I was obliged to return to Hanover to repair and dry the clothes and scenery. I remained and performed one week longer, after which I set out for Fredericktown.

Sept. 5, I performed in Fredericktown, and here I finisht the season.

1812, commenced my theatrical summer business at Hagerstown at the coffee house keep by Christian Fechtig. In company, F. Durang and wife, Blissett and wife, C. Durang, Jones, Morgan, myself and daughters. Our business was good, but the frequent interruptions of quarrels and slanderous tongue of Mrs. Blissett made the whole summer's business very disagreeable to the whole company, and never certain of one night's performance till the night was accomplish'd. We took cash the first 5 nights— $225; after we took benefits. From this I set off for Chambersburg. I had my own wagon with two horses for my bagage and scenery, and my own carriage and two horses for the use of my own family. Only I always took my son's wife in the carriage with my family. I travelet on horseback; I keep the horse, Cornplanter, for that express purpose. At Chambersburg we took board and lodgings at John Snyder, who keep an inn at the corner opposite to the market. He was the sheriff of that town; he charged 3 dollars for board and 25 cents for each gentleman a day for drink. You had the privilege to drink what liquor and

as much as you pleased. We performed in the brewhouse of
Mr. George Barnetz, an old friend of mine or rather school
fellow, who gave me the loan of the place through friendship. He had all the inside taken out to make alterations
and stop'd the workmen to accommodate me till I was
done, for which I made him a compliment of a sum, but he
send me half of the money back again. Here we performed
The Forty Thieves, and had a small horse on the stage.

June 13th, from this we set off for Harrisburg by way of
Shippensburg and Carlisle. We performed in Harrisburg
at Mr. Ziegler's Hotel; myself and family board at a
private house, a widow lady's. ⟨*On account of the indisposition of my wife, I closed after a few nights and waited
with heart heavy* [. . .] *to take Mrs. Durang from this
world to a better world.*⟩

Here I closed the season, and set off for Philad'a ater
remaining two weeks with my family in a private life, and
deposited all my bagage with the wagon and theatrical
extablishment with Mr. Wyeth, the printer.[1] It was the
Almighty's will to draw a vail of moarning on myself and
family at this time in Harrisburg. I must speak in the
highest terms of the ladies and gentlemen and citizen in
general of Harrisburg. They have my heart's thanks for the
politeness which they have done me on this occasion. It is a
just due to them to say they are a religious, humane,
charitable, and of brotherly love, in particular to strangers.
Mr. Wyeth, this gentleman keeps a library, a book store,
and printing establishment, is of exalted good character

and who has proved my sincere friend. My prayers that God may preserve in prosparity, health, and plenty the city and inhabitants of Harrisburg.

I travelet to Philad'a in my carriage with my daughters, my son Ferdinand and wife. I joined the Philad'a theatre this winter, and taught a school in company with Mr. Joseph Harris at Harmony Hall. After the season in Baltimore, I set out on my summer scheme.

1813, June 13, commenced the season in the ball room of Mr. Frederick Hyneman Hotel, Harrisburg. I had in company besides my sons and daughters, Mrs. F. Durang, Mrs. Jacobs, Mr. Carrol.

July 14, performed six nights at Lancaster at Mr. Wentz's Hotel, Queen Street.

August 2d, performed at Peter Wilt's in Yorktown, 9 nights.

August 17, performed at Peter Eckert in Hanover, 12 nights.

Sept. 8th, performed at Gettisburg at a hotel kept by Mr. Keefer, 7 nights, good houses.

Sept. 21, performed at Petersburg at the Indian Queen Hotel keep by Mr. Jacob Brothers, 5 nights, full houses. Here I closed this summer's season and left all my baggage and carriage in the care of Peter Eckert in Hanover till the next season, and travelt on to Baltimore in my wagon.

1814, I collected my theatrical establishment and opened this season in Lancaster with a company of my own family, sons and daughters, Mr. and Mrs. Blisset, Mr. Caulfield, Miss White, Mr. Sheneman, Mr. G. and Ed. Cole. Performed 20 nights in 6 weeks. On the 4th of July I illuminated 13 of the theatre windows with transparencies. At my benefit I took $80.40 ct. I got up for the first time *Perry's Victory*. Performed here during the harvest frolic.

August 5th, performed at Mr. Hyneman's in Harrisburg, 11 nights.

August 29th, performed in Yorktown at Wilt's. Charles and Ferdinand Durang and Geo. Cole entered as volunteers in Harrisburg, and march on to York and were encamped with 5 regiments on south side of Yorktown. From this the whole march'd to Baltimore to the battle of North Point.[2]

At this time all the country towns were left desolate of men; most all had march'd to the seat of war. While the army lay in Yorktown, I assisted in making cartridges in the court house, and after the army had march off I plan a project to draw to gether what people was yet remaining. I gave an exhibition of fireworks in front of my theatre. It being entire noval in York, the rockets was such an astonishing sight and wonder that all the inhabitents assembled, old and young, rich and poor, and so much pleased at the fireworks that when the firework was done I lid up the theatre and it was crowded on the same evening. And here I closed the season and set off for Baltimore with my family and left all my baggage in the care of Peter Witt till the next season.

1815, June 16th, I commencet the season at Yorktown. I

had in company Mr. Horton and wife. We performed 7 nights.

June 28, performed in Harrisburg at Hyneman's Hotel, 13 nights to good houses. During this season the citizens of Harrisburg celebrated the 4th of July in a manner I never witnesset before. It was all sociability and harmony, without distinction, rich and poor: the whole appeared independence, liberty, and equality. All march'd in social bands to a pleasent spot situate on a hill in a wood near the north end of the town, where a colation of all kind of refreshment were provided, with fix'd tables and benches, bars and store rooms, an appropriate canopy decorated with the ensign and banners of America elevated for the President and officers of the day. On the opposide the orchestra, the guests or rather the citizens sat in a circle devided by the canopy and orchestra. All the young gentlemen of the town who could perform on any instrument of music play'd. I joined them with my band and play'd appropriate airs to each toast. An ordnance was fired on occasions. At an early hour in the afternoon the whole march'd through all the principle streets in social band, and retired in good order and harmony. In the evening I illuminated all the windows with thirteen transparencies and the theatre was crowded that night.

The next day a numorous class of ladies celebrated the 4th of July on the same ground. They collected in select parties and walk in procession with music to the appointed place. Some of the old gentlemen of the city attended on them as protectors. But their entertainment surpased the men's of the preceding day. In the afternoon they had a ball on the green; at an early hour they all march'd in procession in town, and several balls were given in the evening, and the "Star Spangled Banner" was sung in many companies. From this town we set out for Carlisle, crossed the lower ferrey in a flat boat with the carriage and wagon.

August 2nd, I erected a theatre in Carlisle at a house [in] the east end of the town, Sign of Perry, keep by a John Kernan, an Irishman. The landlord and landlady took great pains to treat us well, in particular their table was the best that we meet with in any boarding house in our travels. We made money and they made a grate deal of money so that our stay was a great object to them. The landlord and wife were pressing me to stop longer. I spun and harass'd the season as long as I possibly could make out a bill, but I could not preval on the performers to study a line more, tho' it was for there interest too. So that I was obliged to pack up to start for the next town.

When it was seen that I was preparing to go, Mrs. Horton entered in a confederacy with the landlord and landlady to stop my departure. It was a diabolical league and if I could have proved it to a certainty I would have applied to the law for satisfaction. They stole the swingle tree from the baggage wagon and cut the two large braces of the carriage body and all the leather braces of the swingle trees and breast from the tongue of the carriage.

With all this they could not keep me. It took a half a day of constant perseverance to have all mended and made fit to travel. I had blacksmith, saddler, and wheelwrights to work. By the manner of their threats and whole conduct of this day myself and family began to be alarm'd. I did not think our lives safe in this low Irish house. I got my family in the carriage, with the wagon in the street. My family trembled with the dread of being assaulted by these low Irish. O, what a transport of joy it was to us when we found ourselves out of town with our lives safe. The low class of Irish are the most vulgar, savage, and insulting people in America of this town I speak, but the gentry or first class are as polite, humane, and as good in every respect as any in America, and they stand in the same dread and fear of the low Irish who live among them, and are often play'd the same devilish tricks by them. After performing two weeks every night, I travel'd on to Chambersburg by way of Shippensburg. Here I stop'd to refresh. The gentlemen of Shippensburg wish'd me to stop and perform, but I considered the town too small to make it worthwhile.

August 28th, I performed in Chambersburg 2 weeks. I converted a coachmaker's shope in to a theatre, for which I paid $20 a week. I closed the theatre for the season, and made an exhibition of firework which I display'd in an elivated lot joining the west end of the town granted to me by Mr. Shyock. This gentleman was a particular friend to me; he offered me the lot to build the theatre on. I got sixty dollars by the fireworks. I deposited all my theatrical baggage and wagon with Allbright at his house and mill about 3 quarters of a mile from town to the north, to remain till the next season. From this I travel'd with my family in my carriage to Baltimore, over the mountain by way of Gettisburg, Petersburg, Reistertown, Winchester, Hookstown, home.

1816, July 16th. This was my last season of my entering in any more country schemes. By this time I was well weary of the business, principally on account of the performers, who were the chief cause to make it so by their ungratefulness. Their discontent, their eregularities, was more than a man could put up with long.

July 16, I opened the season in Chambersburg at the coachmaker's shop. I paid $20 a week rent and $5 license for each night to the corporation. I performed eleven nights; took $451, expense $191.

I had in company beside my own family Mr. and Mrs. Savage, Mrs. Foster, Mr. King, and Mr. [. . .]. I first boarded at Col. Snider's, Sign of the Eagle, but they did not treat me and my family well enough for the money I paid them. Besides the house was resorted by gamblers and we were obliged to set at the same table with them. Besides they lamed one of my horses in the stable by cutting a deep hole in his shoulder. They refused me assistance to cure the horse or give any kind of satisfaction. He took the privilege of the bar of the theatre and admitted all his relations without the least recompence, but charged me well for every thing. So I left Mr. Col. Snider's house in good time.

I took boarding with my family at Mr. Allbright's, the miller, near town, where we was very pleasentley situated at $9 a week for the whole family. Our room was on the first floor fronting a large orchard where I past sometimes with my gun. We had a well stock'd dairy which the family had the privilege to take refreshments at their pleasure. Near the plantation is a delightfull woods in which the performers of my company would retire into, to study their parts. I myself pass'd many hour in this wood in study. Adjoining was a mill dam wherein are a variety of fish and ducks. In short it is the best place for sportsmen about Chambersburg, and we passed many an agreeable hour at this mill and plantation of Mr. Allbright's.

August 19th, I erected a theatre in the ball room at a hotel keep by Mr. Brown, a stage house in Hagerstown. I paid him $20 a week rent and $5 license to the corporation for each night's performance. We performed every night to full houses attended by the first class. I boarded with my family at a hotel keep by Mr. Irvin, the corner opposide to the market, the genteelest and best entertainment I meet with in my travels. Mr. and Mrs. Irvin in particular deserve my greatest praise and esteeme; they are truly worthy.

After I closed the theatre I took my family in a carriage to visit the cave 9 miles from Hagerstown, which is well worth to see. We dined at a tavern near the cave and returned home. Next morning we set off for Fredericktown. We stop'd at Boomsberry between the two mountains to refresh. Fredericktown, I erected a theatre at a hotel keep by Mr. Hughsten. We boarded in the same house. Mr. Hughsten and family are obliging and genteel; we lived with satisfaction and harmony in this house. We performed two weeks to good success, at the end of which part of the company revolted. The refractory were Mr. and Mrs. Savage, Mrs. Fauster, and Mr. [. . .]. They proposed to give a concert at Mrs. Kimble's and by that scheme to crush the contented part of the company and raise the town against me. But as I allways keep'd provided against such storms, I put out bills for two nights, which to their great astonishment they were not aware of. It was a double bill crowded with favorite entertainments and novalty such as I knew would draw and please. The remaining company, which was my sons and family and Mr. King, they all exerted to the utmost. I brought out *The Attack on Fort McHenry* with the bombardment by the British fleet to crowded houses. The other party gave up the idea of their concert and left the town; they proceeded on to the westward. After I closed the season I set off for Baltimore with my family and company, takeing all my theatrical apparatus home, and here I took leave of all country schemes for the future. If I had allways only confined myself to a small company of my own family we would have been more happy and better paid for our labour.

1817, July 10th, commenced an entertainment for the summer season at the Pavilion Garden in Baltimore on shares, with Mr. Coleman, myself, and F. Durang; Mr. Finley, proprietor. The entertainments consisted of a concert by a full band of music arranged in a large orchestra in front of the stage, the stage decorated with scenery and drapery, the garden and pavilion well lighted up with glass tumblers,[3] skye and signal rockets to announce the night, songs, dances, recitations on the stage. The evening was allways concluded by transparencies or an exhibition of fireworks. To the great praise and credid to Mr. Finley, this is the best regulated garden in America.

1817, August 9th, The great fload occur'd in Baltimore. The excessive rain caused an overflow of the falls and all the waters and streams about and in Baltimore. The overflow of wather accumulated in the country as far as Yorktown, rushing down from the mountains causing great destruction of the farms, mills, and cattle in the country. The fload rush'd in torrent from the north down the falls, sweeping and bringing with its current houses, stables, mills, bridges, fences, trees, wagons, wood, furniture, horses, cows, hogs, &c. The citizens could render no assistance. It was a grand and awful spectacle. Many of the street in Baltimore were over fload one story high. Boats were made use of to relieve the people from their houses out of the second story. All the bridges in Baltimore were destroyed, but the centere one. I received some damage at the pavilion in the destruction of some of my property I had left there, besides prevented of performing for three weeks.

1819, Sept. 2d, I was obliged to leave Baltimore with my family on account of the yellow fever. The steam boat landed us at Camden where we was obliged to stay in quarantine till relieved by the health officers of Philad'a. This happened to be a day of mirth. Hundreds of the Philad'a citizen crossed over to Camden to see a balloon go up, which failed. There are some handsome pleasure gardens in Camden as I have seen in America.

Soon after this a balloon was to ascend out of Vauxhall Garden in Philad'a, but it failed. Thousands of the citizen were disappointed; and enraged mob pull'd down the fences, threw stones, broke and tore everything with the balloon to pieces. Then to glut and compleat their diabolical work set fire to the Vauxhall Theatre and the whole property was consumed by a set of people who are a disgrace to any city or country.

1820, March 30th, on Easter Sunday the theatre in Chesnut Street was set on fire on the stage and the whole burnt. Messrs. Wood and Warren have taken a lease of the Olympic Theatre for ten years, and have done it up in a very hansome style, and altered from what it was before. And opened on Friday Nov. 10 with a good prospect of good business. The performers' salary was reduced to two thirds.

January 24 and 25, the coldest days experienced for many winters. The river froze and have had 9 snows.

On Friday the 8th of January, 1821, the great Mr. Kean [4] from England made his first appearance in *Richard 3d*. He is reported to be the best actor of the day. It was a most fortunate circumstance for the theatrical business in

America. Mr. Kean's presence in the American theatres, which was fast on the decline, but he has raised it in estimation with the public to be respectable, and convinced the spectators to hold the mirror up to nature is to improve the mind, refine the taste, and mend the morals.

On Wedesday, Feb'y 21, 1821, Mr. and Mrs. Barns from the New York theatre made their first appearance in *Romeo and Juliet*, engaged for 7 nights. Poor houses. On Wednesday morning between 3 and 4 o clock, May the 9th 1821, the old theatre in South Street was set on fire and burnt down. Built in 1760 by David Douglas.[5]

Notes

Part One

1. A "proprietary regiment" which later supplied mercenaries for the regiment commanded by the Comte de Deux-Ponts in the American Revolution. See p. xx and note 6.
2. Jacob Durang is referred to in legal documents as both barber and hairdresser. Apparently in the colonies the division of the craft of barber-surgeon into distinct corporations decreed by George II in 1745 had not taken effect.
3. Fairs were held in the High Street in York twice yearly, in June and in November.
4. Perhaps itinerant peddlers who displayed their wares on benches ("settles").
5. Jacob Durang enlisted in First Battalion, York County Militia, December 27, 1775.
6. The French forces arrived in Philadelphia August 15, 1781, but stayed only one day en route to Yorktown. See *Les Combattants Français de la guerre Américaine*, Paris, 1903, p. 223. "The soldiers of the Deux-Ponts regiment found many relatives in Philadelphia, who came to see them in camp. That necessitated our doubling our efforts to prevent desertion, for there are many of them who would prefer to seek their fortune in this country. I was assured that one-tenth of the city was

German and that in the county of Lancaster . . . all the inhabitants were German." *The Revolutionary Journal of Baron Ludwig von Closen,* trans. and ed. Evelyn M. Acomb, Chapel Hill, 1948, p. 120. See also p. 116.

7. Southwark Theater, erected in 1766 and partially destroyed by fire in 1821.

8. A recent arrival from Europe, Templeman had performed in Virginia before opening at the Southwark on February 23, 1780. (Greenwood, *The Circus,* p. 52. Pollock, *The Philadelphia Theatre,* gives his name as Templeton.)

9. Dennis Ryan joined Thomas Wall in the management of a Baltimore-based troupe in 1783. Durang may have seen them in the spring of that year.

10. A dance step executed in part by jumping up and striking the legs together.

11. A member of one of the first companies to come to America from the West Indies. Her debut with Ryan took place in New York, October 18, 1783.

12. Since the first Lewis Hallam died before David Douglass joined the Old American Company, Durang must be referring to the Southwark (1766), which replaced Douglass' first theater, erected in 1760. Lewis Hallam the Younger played principal roles in Douglass' company.

13. Brattle Street Church, presided over by the Rev. Samuel Cooper.

14. A type of boot with uppers of light-colored leather.

15. From the Theatre Royal Edinburg, Allen joined with the younger Hallam in presenting a miscellaneous entertainment. The comic "Lecture upon Heads" had been originally devised and performed by George Alexander Stevens at the Haymarket in London, January 8, 1755. It was freely plagiarized by Stevens' contemporaries and successors.

16. A canvas sheet tightly stretched on a frame, a primitive trampoline.

17. Since the authors of eighteenth-century pantomimes are

rarely identified, and since American versions frequently are (from Durang's own accounts) what we would call today "improvisational," no attempt has been made at attributions.

18. Charles Willson Peale organized an exhibit of paintings and transparencies in 1781; by 1792 it was one of Philadelphia's most popular places of resort.

19. *The Roman Father* by William Whitehead, first performed at Drury Lane in 1750. This play was the principal entertainment on the night of Durang's debut as a dancer.

20. John Henry had made his debut as a comedian at the Southwark in 1767. He was in Jamaica during the Revolution, returning to the States in 1782 and becoming Hallam's partner in 1785.

21. "Ranger" in *The Suspicious Husband* by Benjamin Hoadley (1746).
    "Marplot" in *The Busybody* by Susannah Centlivre (1709).

22. "Sir Peter Teazle" in *The School for Scandal* by R. B. Sheridan (1777).
    "Major O'Flaherty" in *The West Indian* by Richard Cumberland (1771).
    "Patrick" in *The Poor Soldier* by John O'Keeffe (1783).

23. Joseph Harper, light comedian, later manager of theaters in Boston.
    "Charles Surface" in *The School for Scandal*.
    "Bob Acres" in *The Rivals* by R. B. Sheridan (1775).
    "Puff" in *The Critic* by R. B. Sheridan (1779).

24. Stephen Wools, from Bath, performed with the Hallam company primarily in singing roles.
    "Captain Belville" in *Rosina* by Frances Brooke (1782).
    "Hecate" (a singing witch) in *Macbeth*.

25. Charles Biddle seems to have joined the company in March, 1789. His line was character comedy.

26. Thomas Wignell was the first great comic star of the American stage. He made his debut in New York in 1785, became

co-manager of the Philadelphia Chestnut Street Theater in 1794. The son of a minor English itinerant actor, he created the role of Jonathan in *The Contrast* by Royall Tyler (1787), the first native American play to be produced after the Revolution.

"Joseph Surface" in *The School for Scandal*.

"Darby" in *The Poor Soldier*, and also in *Darby's Return*, a reworking of O'Keeffe's play by William Dunlap.

27. Heard had appeared in Baltimore in 1782, and with the American company in New York in 1785. His Philadelphia debut was on March 11, 1789. Durang's comment suggests that he was an unreliable colleague.

28. Owen Morris first appeared with Douglass in 1758. Bernard cites him as the earliest performer of old men on the American stage.

"Sir Francis Gripe" in *The Busybody*.

"Lissardo" in *The Wonder* by Mrs. Centilivre.

"Old Rowley" in *The School for Scandal*.

"Sharp" in *The Lying Valet* by David Garrick (1741).

29. J. Robinson made his acting debut in 1790, but he was also a playwright: *Constitutional Follies* (1791) and *The Yorker's Strategem* (1792).

"Careless," "Snake" in *The School for Scandal*.

30. Ryan had been with the company at least since 1789.

31. Gay also was assigned bit parts in large-cast plays.

32. Lake made his debut in New York, 1785.

"Trip" in *The School for Scandal*.

"Father Goodchild" in *Love à la Mode* by Charles Macklin (1759).

"Silk stocking and paper ruffles" describes the conventional costume of the aging dandy.

33. Weston acted only briefly and in minor roles. Charles Durang identifies "Bagatelle Moses" as the character generally called "Moses" in *The School for Scandal*, but he seems to have "married" characters from two plays.

34. Jacob Snyder joined the American Company during their performances in Providence, Rhode Island, 1759.

35. Maria Storer came from Rich's London company to make her debut in New York in 1765. She married Henry in 1773 and was the leading lady of the company in 1789–1790. Although highly regarded as a singer, her capricious and disdainful attitude made her unpopular with audiences.

36. The second wife of Owen Morris, she made her debut October 28, 1772.
"Lady Teazle" in *The School for Scandal*.
"Kathleen" in *Darby's Return*.

37. Mrs. Harper had been in the Old American Company since 1785; her line was comic old women.
"Mrs. Malaprop" in *The Rivals*.
"Ursula" in *The Padlock* by Isaac Bickerstaff (1768).
"Nora" in *Love in a Camp* by O'Keeffe. According to Pollock (p. 148), Mrs. Harper was actually cast as "Flora," while Mrs. Morris played "Nora."

38. Miss Tuke joined the company in 1785. Her marriage to Lewis Hallam occurred about 1794 and was the subject of much rumor and raillery.

39. This was the principal New York home of the American Company, opened December 7, 1769. It is amusingly described by Jonathan in *The Contrast*, Act III, scene 1.

40. Mrs. Fortune was the widow of a Scotch merchant. She was assisted in the operation of her boarding house by her two daughters, Esther (who was to marry William Warren), and Euphemia (who was to marry Joseph Jefferson, founder of an American theatrical dynasty).

41. This was a pageant devised by David Garrick to celebrate the bicentennial of Shakespeare's birth.

42. A primitive magic lantern.

43. This seems to refer to the Kenna family who arrived May 15, 1786. Mrs. Kenna alone was received with respect: "She is unfortunate in being connected with a husband who guz-

zles fat beef,—with a gawky son whose eyes pass and cross under his nose, and whose tongue is red, and with a daughter who ought to beat hemp at Bridewell" (*The Daily Advertiser*, quoted in Odell, *Annals of The New York Stage*, I, 258).

44. The record book of Old St. Joseph's Church, Philadelphia, reads "1787/ Philadelphia/ *January 25/* a Rev. Francis Beeston, tribus promissis publicationibus, Johannes Durang, juvenis C. et Maria McHuin puella C. . . ." The Reverend Martin J. Casey, Pastor of Old St. Joseph's, explains that "C." means "white."

45. Pastor of Old St. Joseph's beginning in 1786.

46. Charles Durang explains that these were incorporate names of "notorious characters"; the ladies were most certainly whores. (Durang, *The Philadelphia Stage*, I, Chap. XIV).

47. *Douglas*, a tragedy by John Home (1757). Dunlap claims for Martin the title of first American-born actor (*A History of the American Theatre*, I, 170). His debut as Norval took place March 13, 1790.

48. Alexander Placide, founder of a celebrated theatrical family, was born in Paris and first achieved theatrical success at Astley's Amphitheater, London, where he was known as "The Great Devil" for his tumbling feats (Greenwood, p. 67). Madame Placide sang in broken English and danced with her husband. Their American debut took place February 3, 1792.

49. Identified as Paulo Redigé in *Bulletin New York Public Library*, LXIV (1960), 478–491.

50. Dunlap was a playwright, painter, diarist, and the first historian of the American stage. He became part manager with Hallam and Hodgkinson in 1796.

51. An elderly fop ("silk stocking and paper ruffles") in *The Clandestine Marriage* by David Garrick and the elder George Colman (1766).

52. Charles Biddle came to America with Henry in 1785. He retired from the stage in 1790.

53. George Easterly founded Vauxhall Gardens at Harrowgate in 1784.

54. These actors are not readily identified. Mr. Vaughan had been with the Old American Company and soon rejoined them; Mr. Kenney made his debut September 24, 1791; it is possible that Johnson had played minor roles with Hallam before the Revolution; Mr. Stewart, a noted pedestrian from New York, was always referred to as "Walking Stewart"; a Mr. Pursell had delivered "Lectures on Heads and Manners" March 12, 1787, at the Long Room, South and Front Streets; a Miss Wells had appeared at the New Theater, July 1, 1795.

55. John Bill Ricketts, "the greatest rider of his day," came from England in 1792, where he had worked with Charles Hughes, manager of a circus whose fame rivaled that of Philip Astley. Ricketts established a riding school at Twelfth and Market Streets in Philadelphia and constructed the first circus in the city. (Greenwood, p. 63.)

56. That is, to perform comic interludes involving equestrian feats.

57. John Hodgkinson, born in Manchester, England, 1767, was known as the "Provincial Garrick" before coming to America in 1792; Mrs. Hodgkinson was a talented actress and singer; William King, a dissipated man, second to Hodgkinson and totally dependent upon him; James West, a minor actor in Bath and Bristol, played chiefly in farces in America; Mrs. Brett, mother of Mrs. Hodgkinson, played comic old women (Durang's memory may be at fault here: Dunlap, I, 283, gives her American debut as Boston, 1795; Pollock does not include her in any Philadelphia companies); Miss Brett was Mrs. Hodgkinson's sister, an unimportant talent—she married King in 1793; Luke Rob[b]ins, a scene painter in Philadelphia, Petersburg, Richmond, and Norfolk, later a teacher of landscape and flower painting; Mrs. Pownall, formerly Mrs. Wrighten of Drury Lane, well known both as an actress and a singer, left her English hus-

band and theater and went to France where she remained until Henry engaged her for America; Prigmore, a low comedian from Jefferson's company at Plymouth; Floar, able and ingenious, according to Charles Durang, but too apt to sacrifice to "the jolly god"; M. Quenet, dancer and creator of the popular pantomime *Daniades;* Madame Guardie first came to America from Paris with Wignell and Reinagle, joining the Old American Company in 1794; Monsieur and Madame Val were French performers engaged to support Madame Guardie; Pellisiere was both composer and performer in the orchestra, later a horn player in the orchestra of the Chestnut Street Theater.

58. In *The Highland Reel* by John O'Keeffe.

59. "Vapid" in *The Dramatist* by Frederick Reynolds (1793); "Puff" in *The Critic* by R. B. Sheridan.

60. Charles S. Powell, Boston actor-manager.

61. Born in 1774, grandfather of the great interpreter of Rip Van Winkle. He had come to America to join Powell's Boston company in 1795; when Powell failed, Jefferson joined Hallam and Hodgkinson as a scene painter and comedian.

62. Mr. Marriot, from Edinburgh, first joined the company in 1794; Mrs. Marriot wrote plays and farces without much success; Mr. Crosby, an Irish baronet, whose stage name was Richards; Mr. Hamilton played comic old men; Mr. Seymour seems to have been of little consequence; his wife is described as beautiful, talented, and illiterate; Patterson had been with Lindsey and Wall in Baltimore, 1782—later he danced with Harper at Newport, 1794, and at Charlestown, 1795; Mr. and Mrs. Rankin had been with the company since 1791, Miller joining in 1793—Mrs. Rankin shortly became Mrs. Miller and the next year they were playing at Charlestown.

63. According to Greenwood (p. 71) the clown at Rickett's circus in 1795 was William Sully, father of the famous artist Thomas. William's second son, Matthew, also went on the stage.

64. Francis Ricketts, John's brother, an accomplished equestrian. Thomas Franklin, clown from London's Royal Circus.
65. Signora Spinacuta, equestrienne who rode two horses at full gallop.
66. Mr. and Mrs. Chambers were former members of the American Company, originally singers at the Royalty and Haymarket Theaters, London.
67. "A Magnificent Representation of the Siege of Gaza, Battle of Arabela, and the Triumphant Entry of Alexander the Great into the City of Babylon" (Pollock, p. 383).

Part Two

1. Cornplanter (named for the Senecan chief), a trick horse that could ungirth and remove his own saddle and leap over another horse fifteen hands high (Greenwood, p. 71).
2. *The Tailor,* a famous interlude of comic riding, first introduced by Philip Astley. Originally called "Billy Button, or the Tailor's Ride to Brentford," successive clowns developed their own versions, the earliest in America (1785) being, "The Taylor humorously riding to New York." (*Pennsylvania Packet,* August 15, 1785.)
3. Composed by Phile (or Feyles), it was first performed April 21, 1789, when Washington crossed the bridge at Trenton en route to his inauguration in New York. (*The Diary of George Washington, from 1789 to 1791* . . . , ed. Benson J. Lossing, Richmond, 1861, under the date November 24, 1790.)
4. A thin pile of blankets, furs, or clothing.
5. Coarse fabric combining cotton and wool.
6. Probably a waiting room.
7. *The Death of Captain Cook*—"Grand Serious Pantomime"; *Robinson Crusoe, or Harlequin Friday,* a pantomime dubiously attributed to Sheridan.
8. A Portuguese coin (Johannes), worth about $8.
9. Simon McTavish (1750–1804), one of the original partners

in the Northwest Company, a syndicate of fur-traders; Joseph Frobisher (1740–1810) went into partnership with McTavish in 1787, the partners becoming chief suppliers and virtual directors of the company.

10. A farce taken from *Man Bewitched* by Mrs. Centlivre.
11. At Old Tappen, near Tarrytown, New York, on the east bank of the Hudson river.

Part Three

1. The state capital from 1799–1812.
2. Thomas McKeon, the fourth governor of Pennsylvania, had been elected to the office for the first time in October 1799. A playbill announcing his intention to visit Durang's "fit-up" is dated January 2, 1800 and locates the theater as in the White Horse Tavern, East King Street. The program promises: "Pantomime, Singing, Hornpipe *Dancing*, Tumbling, SPEAKING, &c. &c. And in particular an Indian WAR and SCALP Dance by Mr. Durang and Mr. F. Ricketts."
3. Durang opened the South Street on May 1, 1800, with "The Thespian Panorrama." A group of amateurs (The Thespian Society) challenged his right to their title but he held on for eleven nights of both protean and herculean performances on his own part: tumbling, dancing, "speaking" (Jaques on "The Seven Ages of Man" or Goldsmith's "Epilogue"), and staging pantomime and farce (Reese, *Cradle of Culture*, pp. 26–28).
4. Cornbread in the form of small cakes (pones).
5. See the Appendix.
6. See the Appendix.
7. That is, Mennonites and German Baptist Brethren.
8. John Spayd (1764–1822), Charles Evans (1768–1847).
9. The Columbia Garden was on Market Street above Thirteenth.

10. Rohrer's Ball Room, Lancaster.
11. A "display of optical illusions which introduces the phantoms or apparitions of the dead or absent in a way more completely illusive than has ever yet been witnessed" (Reese, p. 100).

Part Four

1. John Wyeth, printer of *The Oracle of Dauphin* and *Harrisburg Advertiser*, also builder and proprietor of Shakespeare House, a hotel and theater combined.
2. September 12, 1814.
3. "Hurricane lamps."
4. Edmund Kean visited America in 1820 and 1825. If his first visit justified Durang's pious statement, his second was catastrophic.
5. The following is written on the page after this entry and appears to be in John Durang's handwriting.

In 1808, Mrs. Anne Warren died.
[In] 1809, John E. Harwood, age 39 years.
November 18, 1809, Giles Leonard Barrett, [age] 65.
Lewis Hallam, at Phil'a, South 5th St., 1 November 1808, 68 years, or 73.

While playing at the old South Street in 1808 (summer) old Hallam related to me the first company's coming out in 1752 from London to Virginia in the ship called the *Charming Salley* (Capt. Lee). They [had] 6 weeks passage to York town, Virginia. They opened at Williamsburgh with the *Merchant of Venice* and 'Garrick's *Lethe* in September 1852 [*sic*].

Prologue writ by Singleton—Spoken by Rigby
Cast of the play:

Bassanio — Mr. Rigby
Antonio — Clarkson
Gratiano — Singleton
Lancelot and Tubal —
  Hallam
Shylock — Malone

Salereo and Duke — Herbert
Servant to Portia — Hallam,
  Jun. (being his 1st appear-
  ance on any stage)
Portia — Mrs. Hallam
Jessica — Miss Hallam
Nerissa — Miss Palmer

Appendix to the Notes

Mr. William Warren—Born in Bath, May 10, 1767. Died in Washington, D.C., October 19, 1832. Married Mrs. Merry (Mrs. Wignell) and managed Chestnut. Philadelphia debut December 5, 1796, as Friar Laurence. Listed as coming from the Theatre, York.

Mr. Moreton (John Pollard)—Born near Saratoga, New York. Died of consumption, Philadelphia, April 2, 1798. Was engaged by Wignell in England after working in a Calcutta counting house. Leading high comedian.

Mr. Chalmers—Born in England. Came to U.S., 1793. Died in England, 1806. Genteel comedian. "Originally a Harlequin, he could never play a part without a jump or a turn in it." (Durang, I, Chap. xxi.)

Mr. Charles Whitlock—Born in England. Died there, 1812. Had long been provincial actor and manager in England before Wignell brought him over. Excellent in heavy fathers.

Mr. Francis—Born in England. U.S. debut 1793 as a dancer. Appeared with Rickett's Circus in New York. Died in Philadelphia of gout, 1826. Dancer and pantomimist with W & R company. Tag in *The Spoiled Child* by Bickerstaff.

Mr. Green—Seems to have played old character parts. Later manager of Richmond, Norfolk theaters. Died 1816.

Mr. Marshal—Good in fops and Frenchmen. Also principal tenor in opera. Died in England, 1816.

Mr. Darly—Born in England. Died there, 1819. Had been Covent Garden favorite as a singer. Originally a bucket-maker, and never a very good actor.

Mr. Francis Blissett—Son of Blissett, the Bath comedian. Never acted in England. Dr. Caius in *Merry Wives of Windsor*. Jerry Sneak in *Mayor of Garratt* (farce by Foote). Sheepface in *Village Lawyer* by McCready.

Mr. (John) Bernard—1756–1828. Excellent comedian from England. Debut in Philadelphia, December 11, 1797. See his autobiography, *Retrospections of America 1797–1811*.

Mr. (James) Fennel—Born in London, December 11, 1766. Educated Eton and Trinity College, Cambridge. Died in Philadelphia, June, 1816. Had played leads at Covent Garden prior to Philadelphia debut. Leading man of company. Left company for a time to go into home salt manufacture. Appeared at Park Theatre in New York in 1800 and again in 1802. He was always erratic and reckless, which kept him from attaining the high position to which his acting entitled him.

Mr. Gross—One of players secured by Warren in England in 1805.

Mr. (John) Darley, Jr.—Debut February, 1794, at New Theatre. Danced. Went into army but returned to the stage in 1800. Fine singer, good in comedy and as second gentlemen in drama.

Mr. A. Warrel, Senior—Engaged by Wignell, with his wife and two sons, in 1793. Not good actor, but family useful in filling out a cast. Minor roles in operas.

Two Messrs. Warrell, Junior—Thomas, a very good dancer; James, dancer, later scene painter.

Mr. L'Estrange—Brought over by Wignell in 1796. Debut at New Theatre December 5, 1796, with wife and daughter. Had been with Covent Garden. Debut in Philadelphia as Capulet. Basically prompter. Died 1804.

Mr. (Charles) Milbourn—An experienced scene painter from London. Played clown in *Birth of Harlequin* during first season at New Theatre. First appearance July 17, 1794.

Mr. (John Joseph) Holland—Born in London, 1776, came to Philadelphia, 1796.

Signeior Doctor—Signior Joseph Doctor, an acrobat imported from Sadlers Wells in 1795 to help Wignell compete with Ricketts.

Mr. Byrn(e)—James Byrne had been imported from Covent Garden in 1796 to do pantomimes and comic operas (Pollock). T. A. Brown (*History of the American Stage*) says his name was Oscar, that he was born in England, and that he made his debut at Annapolis in 1793. His debut, in Philadelphia, however (December 7, 1796), is listed as his "First Appearance in America."

Mr. Hardinge—Philadelphia debut December 20, 1797. English; brought over by Wignell.

Mr. Gillingham—Leader of the orchestra, "the celebrated violinist from London" (Pollock, I, 35).

Ladies

Mrs. (Ann) Merry—Known in England as Miss Brunton, was born in 1769, and first acted at Bath in 1785. In 1792 she left the stage and married Mr. Robert Merry. When his means failed, they accepted a tempting offer from America, and Mrs. Merry made her debut at New Theatre, Philadelphia, as Juliet on December 5, 1796. Mr. Merry died in 1798, and in 1805 his widow married Mr. Wignell, who lived only seven weeks after the wedding. In 1806 she married Mr. Warren. She died at Alexandria in 1808.

Mrs. (Charles) Whitlock—Was Eliza Kemble, the youngest sister of Mrs. Siddons. Married Whitlock in June, 1785. The chief attraction of Newcastle Circuit. Philadelphia debut February

19, 1794, in Southerne's *Isabella*. Born April 2, 1761. Died in England, 1835.

Mrs. Shaw—Was hired for the comic old women. Fat; not too well known. Her husband played the hautboy in the orchestra as he had at Drury Lane. Debut in Philadephia as Lady Waitford in *The Dramatist*, December 21, 1794, at the New Theatre.

Mrs. Warrel(l)—Esteemed singer at Bath. Covent Garden, 1790–1791. Brighton, Edinburgh, 1792–1793. Debut December 17, 1794, as Victoria in *The Castle of Andalusia*.

Mrs. Oldmixon (Miss George)—Seilhamer (*History of the American Theatre*) calls her "The most distinguished member of Mr. Wignell's company." Had performed with great success at Drury Lane and Haymarket before coming to America in 1794. Wife of Sir John Oldmixon, memoirist. Noted as a singer. Debut May 14, 1794, in Germantown as Clarinda in *Robin Hood*. Retired; established girls' school.

Mrs. Byrn(e)—Came with her husband in 1796 to do pantomimes and comic operas for Wignell.

Mrs. Francis—Wife of William Francis. At New Theatre from first season. Born in London. Died in Philadelphia, 1834. (Dunlap, I, 234.)

Mrs. Doctor—Wife of Joseph Doctor the acrobat. Began playing small parts but eventually was raised to secondary roles.

Mrs. Warren—This is either Mrs. Merry after 1803 or the lady playing minor roles in the 1798/1799 season.

Mrs. Gillingham—Singer and wife of a musical director.

Miss Milbourne—Daughter of scene painter. Debut January 2, 1795.

Mrs. Bernard (Miss Fisher)—Second wife of John Bernard (1795). Died 1805. Debut January 26, 1798, as Cicely Copsley in *The Will* by Reynolds.

Mrs. Hardinge—Second lady for comedy or tragedy (Dunlap, I, 369). Born in England, emigrated with husband. Debut December 22, 1797, at New Theatre as Lady Eleanor Irwin in Mrs. Inchbald's *Every One Has His Fault*.

Mrs. Marshal(1)—Formerly at Covent Garden. Came over with husband for Wignell's first season. Petite; capable actress and singer. Later left company and returned as Mrs. Wilmot. (Dunlap, I, 234.)

Mr. Strickland—Master Carpenter, father to famous architect.

Performers who have since joined the Company

Mr. (Thomas Abthorpe) Cooper—Born in England, 1776. Educated by William Godwin. With the aid and advice of Thomas Holcroft, the author of *The Road to Ruin* and a close friend of Godwin's, Cooper went on the stage at the age of seventeen, beginning at Edinburgh without success. Afterwards he acted at London, and on December 9, 1796, made his first appearance in America as Macbeth in the New Theatre. In 1806 he became manager of the Park Theatre, New York. Last New York appearance was in 1835. Afterwards he performed in the South. Died in Bristol, Pennsylvania, April 21, 1849.

Mr. Twaits—Born in Birmingham, England, April 25, 1781. Died in New York City, August 22, 1814. First acted at Waltham Abbey, England. Brought over by Wood for Philadelphia in 1803. (Dunlap, II, 216–218.) A fine comic actor.

Mr. McKenzie—Very good in heavy tragedy (Wood, *Personal Recollections,* p. 153).

Mr. (Spencer) Cone—Was a member of New Theatre in 1807. Later retired from acting and went into the ministry. Died in New York City, September 4, 1855. Played juvenile tragedy and second men of comedy very respectably.

Mr. Fulenton—Good as serious father (Wood, p. 84).

Mr. (Alexander) Cain—Born in Deptford, England. Raised in Burlington, New Jersey. Considered Wood's rival in Philadelphia. Died June 12, 1808.

Mr. Robins—Scene painter.

Mr. Bray—From Royal York Theatre, 1805.

Mr. Duff—John Duff of London and Dublin. American debut in

Boston. Came to Philadelphia, 1811/12 season. Made debut in *Macbeth* and leads in farce.

(Charles) Durang—John Durang's son, born 1796. See the Introduction.

(Ferdinand) Durang—John Durang's son. See the Introduction.

(Joseph) Harris—Stepson of William Francis, prompter.

(Thomas) Scrivenor (Scrivener)—Nephew to Mrs. Francis, prompter, and played minor roles.

Usher—Skillful in the portrayal of cruel uncles and heavy villains.

(Joseph) Saymour (Seymour)—From New York Theatre (Wood). Joseph Seymour died September 30, 1814.

Burk—Joined Chestnut Street with wife in 1817. Had been with Commonwealth Company and Park Theatre, New York City.

Prigmore—See note 57, p. 150.

McFarland—Vocalist from Boston.

Jones—Mr. and Mrs. Jones came during the 1802/3 season. Mr. Jones failed to gain favor. (Wood, p. 84.)

Hathwell—Came in fall of 1815.

Bailey—With company in 1806/7 season.

Mr. (Giles Leonard) Barrett—Joined company in 1807. His son, Master George Barrett, "The Young American Roscius," became popular in Philadelphia for high comedy.

(James William) Wallack—New York debut September 7, 1818, as Macbeth.

(John) Martin—Joined the American Company in 1790 playing the young leads in comedy and tragedy.

Jones—Came from England with wife in the summer of 1801. Good in sentimental comedy.

Anderson—Son-in-law of Jefferson, but a poor actor.

Jacobs—Born in England. American debut at Charleston Theatre. Philadelphia debut March 4, 1808. A clever vocalist, but no actor.

T. Jefferson—Thomas, son of Joseph.

Stuard—See note 54, p. 149.

Robinson—Called himself "The Antipodean Whirligig." In addition to standing on his head and performing his whirligig act, he gave remarkable imitations of bird calls, tumbled, and did comic pantomime. Joined company in 1801.

Wilmot—Joined company in 1807.

Hopkins—Made successful debut as Tony Lumpkin and became popular in the South (Wood, p. 67).

(Charles) Sharnock—Prompter, also singing actor.

(Louis) Mestayer—Frenchman who played small French parts very well. Excellent pantomimist.

(Andrew Jackson) Allen—Born December 10, 1776. Debut in New York, 1787. Debut in Philadelphia, November 13, 1810. Retired from the stage and became costumer with Edwin Forrest. Died October 29, 1853.

(John D.) Miller—Native New Yorker. Debut 1796. Retired from the stage to join his brother in business.

(Leigh) Waring—From Dublin and Liverpool theaters. Debut April 20, 1813, at the Southwark. Charles Durang describes him as a "vivid and dashing light comedian." Later engaged at Chestnut Street. Married Caroline Durang.

Green—Really one of original company. Later managed several southern theaters.

(Owen) Morris—Original member of company. See note 28, p. 146.

Johnson—Debut November 27, 1815, as Captain Dudley in *The West Indian.*

(Don) Lopez—Prompter.

Doyel (Doyle)—From New York.

Mrs. Seymour—From New York, 1804/5 season.

Mrs. Melmouth—Debut with company December 4, 1805. A famous villainess in tragedies.

Mrs. Solomon—Joined Chestnut Street company in 1796. Her daughters sang with her. They later joined the Boston company.

Mrs. Jones—Came 1802/3 season. "Had exquisite voice and much cultivation" (Wood, p. 84).

Mrs. Barrett—Wife of Giles and mother of George. Actress "of much provincial celebrity" (Wood, p. 97).

Blissett's good wife—See p. 117.

Miss C. and K. Durang—Daughters of John Durang; see the Introduction.

Mrs. Darley—Formerly Miss E. Westray. Popular ingenue. At Boston Haymarket with her two sisters and her stepparents, the Simpsons, in 1796–1797.

Mrs. Jefferson—Debut December 30, 1803, as Rosaura in *She Would and She Would Not.*

Mrs. Anderson—Wife of business manager of Chestnut Street Theatre. A singer who stayed with the company until 1823.

Mrs. Jacobs—Formerly, Miss Pettit. Left company in 1812 to join Olympic company in New York.

Mrs. Simpson—An English provincial actress. She made her Philadelphia debut September 19, 1811. Mother of Westray girls who became Mrs. Darley, Mrs. Wood, and Mrs. Twaits.

Miss White—Pupil of James Fennell, debut September 18, 1811.

Mrs. Mestayer—A dancer and performer on the slackwire.

Mrs. Downie—Joined company in 1803/4 season when her husband returned to the company after three years in Boston. Returned to Boston in 1805, Charleston in 1807, back to Philadelphia, 1809 to 1811. A singer and player of minor parts.

Mrs. Waring—Formerly Caroline Placide.

Mrs. Morris—The second Mrs. Morris. An original member of New Theatre Company. Played leading female roles. Had been with her husband, Owen, at Southwark.

Mr. (James) Entwis(t)le—Debut December 28, 1814. Good actor in comic boys' parts; good at comic songs.

Mrs. Entwis(t)le—Originally Mrs. Mason, comedienne.

Sir John Oldmixon—Grandson of the John Oldmixon included by Pope in *The Dunciad.* Was a Bath beau in the 1780's. Model for Bernard's Lord Sparkle in Mrs. Cowley's *Which Is the*

Man? Came over when wife joined New Theatre and took up gardening to make some extra money.

Mr. Woodham—Musician and singer.

Mrs. Woodham—Debut December 6, 1805. Attractive. Played in comedy and farce.

Mr. (Gilbert) Fox—Former etcher and engraver. Was the first to sing "Hail Columbia." According to Wood, he was bad both at acting and singing (p. 106).

Mr. Rutherford—Recruited by Warren in England in the summer of 1805.

(Benjamin) Webster—A singer.

Harwood—Returned after a six-year absence in 1805. Withdrew in 1806 when he could not get the roles he wanted; returned again in 1809, but died September 21, 1809, age thirtynine.

References

Brown, T. Allston. *History of the American Stage*. 2 vols. New York, 1870.

Carter, W. C., and A. J. Glossbrenner. *History of York County from its Erection to the Present Time*. York (Pa.), 1834.

Diffenderffer, F. R. "Early Lancaster Playbills and Playhouses," *Papers Read Before the Lancaster County Historical Society*, VII (1903), 24–45.

Dunlap, William. *A History of the American Theatre*. New York, 1832.

Durang, Charles. *The Philadelphia Stage, from the Year 1749 to the Year 1855; Partly Compiled from the Papers of His Father, the Late John Durang, with Notes by the Editors* [of the Philadelphia *Sunday Dispatch*]. Philadelphia, 1854.

Fennel, James. *An Apology for the Life of James Fennel*. Philadelphia, 1819.

Greenwood, Isaac John. *The Circus: Its Origins and Growth Prior to 1835*. Dunlap Society Publication No. 5, 1898. Reprinted, New York, 1909.

Morgan, George H. *Annals Comprising Memoirs, Incidents, and Statistics of Harrisburg*. Harrisburg, 1858.

Odell, George C. D. *Annals of the New York Stage*. 15 vols. New York, 1927–1949.

Pollock, Thomas Clark. *The Philadelphia Theatre in the Eighteenth Century*. Philadelphia, 1933.

Reese, Davis James. *Cradle of Culture, 1800–1810: The Philadelphia Stage*. Philadelphia, 1957.

————. "Old Drury of Philadelphia." Ph.D. dissertation, University of Pennsylvania, 1932.

Seilhamer, George O. *History of the American Theatre*. 3 vols. Philadelphia, 1888–1891.

Watson, John F. *Annals of Philadelphia and Pennsylvania in the Olden Time*. Philadelphia, 1856.

Wood, William B. *Personal Recollections of the Stage*. Philadelphia, 1855.

Index

A place name in parentheses is used to distinguish non-theatrical persons from members of the profession. The plays listed on pages 122–126 and the Canadian towns on pages 91–92 are not included in the Index unless they appear elsewhere in the book.

Abbercrombie, Miss, 109
Abbercrombie, Mr., 109
Actors, Durang's opinion of, 116–117
Albany, N.Y., description, 50; citizens, 49–50; circus, 49; fire, 50–51; mentioned, 47, 48, 92
Alexandria, Va., 100, 101, 113
Allbright, Mr. (Chambersburg), 137
Allen, Andrew Jackson, 109, 161
Allen, Mr., 16, 17, 19, 87, 144
Allen, Mrs., 16, 17, 109
Allen, Mr., Jr., 41
Allport, Mrs., 129
Anderson, Mr., 109, 160
Anderson, Mrs., 109, 162
Annapolis, Md., 29, 46, 97, 99, 101, 127
Andre, Major John, 47, 48, 93
Arnold, Benedict, 47
Arnold, Miss, 108

The Attack on Fort McHenry, 139

Bache, Mrs. (Benjamin Franklin's daughter), 9
Bailey, Mr., 109, 160
Baltimore, Md., city springs, 121; flood, 140; Howard's Park, 121; Star-Spangled Banner, xviii; yellow fever, 140; mentioned, xvi, 28, 46, 97, 101, 110, 113, 118, 120, 121, 127, 132, 133, 137, 139
Bandits, 10
Barnitz, George (Chambersburg, 131
Barns, Mr. and Mrs., 142
Barrett, Giles Leonard, 109, 160
Barrett, Mrs., 109, 162
Basin Harbour, Vt., 56
Bassett, Monsieur (Quebec), 85
Bates, Mr., 108

The Battle of the Kegs, 44

Baum, Mr. (Lancaster), 127

Benefit, Durang's first, 29

Bentley, Mr. (Quebec), 87

Bernard, John, 107, 156

Bernard, Mrs., 108, 158

Berthierville, Quebec, 82

Biddle, Charles, 20, 31, 145, 148

Bingham, Mrs. (Philadelphia), 26

Bird, Mr., 44

Bird, L., 47

Birth of Harlequin, or The Witches Frolic, 29

Blanchard, Mr., 9–10

Blissett, Mr., 130, 133

Blissett, Mrs., 109, 117, 130, 133

Blissett, Francis, 107, 156

Boston, Mass., description, 14–15; mentioned, 12, 38–41 *passim*

Brattle Street Church (Boston), 15

Bray, Mr., 108, 159

Bray, Mrs., 109

Brett, Mrs., 36, 149

Brett, Miss, 36, 149

Briars, Mr., 109

Briden, Mr. (Philadelphia), 127

"Bright Phoebus," 32, 33

Brook, Colonel (Harrisburg), 113, 119

Broomly, Mr., 110

Brothers, Jacob (Petersburg), 132

Brown, Mr. (Hagerstown), 138

Burgoyne, General John, 59

Burk, Mr., 109, 160

Busselotte, Charles (Durang's brother-in-law), 19, 34, 35

Busselotte, Mrs. (Catherine Durang), 35

Byrne, James, 108, 157

Byrne, Mrs., 108, 158

Cain, Mr. (Loghouse Pt., N.Y.), 52

Cain, Alexander, 108, 159

Callender, Squire (Vermont), 55

Cambridge, Pa., 98

Camden, N.J., 141

Cammel, Mr., 59

Canada, Durang's tour of, 47–93; opinion of, 88–90; towns visited, 91–92

Canadians, description of, 78–79

Cap Santé, Quebec, 85

Captain Cook, 70

Carlisle, Pa., 120, 128, 129, 131, 135

Carlisle, Mr. (Philadelphia constable), 27

"Carlisle March," 28

Carroll, Mr., 132

Carter, Mr., 109

Carter, Mrs., 109

Caughnawaga, Quebec, 70

Caulfield, Mr., 133

Chalmers, Mr., 107, 155

Chambers, Mr. and Mrs., 44, 151

Chambersburg, Pa., 128, 129, 130, 136, 137

Charlestown, Mass., 15

Chase, Judge Samuel (Baltimore), 28

Chazy, Quebec, 62

"Cherry Charlott's Jigg," 28

Charnock, Mr., 129

Cheeseman, Mr. (St. Johns), 67

Chestnut Street Theatre (Philadelphia), Durang joins, 106;

members of company, 107–109; staff, 112; burns, 141; mentioned, xvii, xix, 37, 95, 105, 106, 110
Chimney Point, Vt., 56
Circus, Durang in, xii, 68–69, 95; *see also* Lailson's Circus, Ricketts' Circus
Clapsadle, Mr. (Hanover), 120
Clark, Simon (Montreal), 67, 73, 76
Cloud, Mr., 109
Coffea, Mrs., 118
Cole, Edward, 133
Cole, George, 133
Coleman, Mr., 139
Columbia Garden (Baltimore), 118, 127
Commings, Mr. (carpenter), 112
Cone, Spencer, 108, 159
Cooper, Thomas Abthorpe, xix, 108, 159
Cornplanter (Ricketts' horse), 47, 151
Cornplanter (Durang's horse), 104, 105, 122, 130
Correy, Miss, 95
Crosby, Mr., 41, 150
Crosbye, Mrs. (wardrobe ass't.), 112
Cross, Mr., 129
Crown Point, N.Y., 56
Cumberlandhead, Vt., 90
Cunningham, Mr., 109
Curry, Miss, 44

Dailey, Mr. (Rouses Point), 61
Dancer, Durang as, 11, 12, 17, 79–80
Dancing schools, 38, 110, 116, 127, 132

Darley, John, 107, 156
Darley, John, Jr., 107, 155
Darley, Mrs., 109, 162
Davis, Mr., 129
Decker, Mr., 28
Decker, Mrs., 95
Deen, Widow (Sandy Hill), 51
De Graft, Mr. (Philadelphia horseman), 105, 118
Delenge, Miss, 108
DeRover, Jemmy (Philadelphia), 8
Doctor, Signor Joseph, 108, 157
Doctor, Mrs., 108, 158
Donaughy, W. (L. Champlain), 57
Donagany, Mr. (Pointe aux Tremble), 81
Douglas (Home), 30
Douglass, David, 12, 142
Downie, Mr., 109
Downie, Mrs., 109, 162
Doyle, Mr., 109, 161
Drummond, Mr., 109, 121
Duff, John, 108, 159–160
Dunlap, William, xii, 31, 38, 43, 148
Durang, Augustus (son), xix, 129
Durang, Catherine (sister), 19
Durang, Charlotte (daughter), xix, 109
Durang, Charles (son), *History of Phila. Stage*, xiv, xviii; mentioned, xvii, xviii, 109, 113, 118, 129, 130, 133, 160
Durang, Edwin Forrest (grandson), xix
Durang, Ferdinand (son), Star-Spangled Banner, xviii; mentioned, xviii, xix, 109, 114, 118, 129, 130, 132, 133, 139

Durang, Jacob (father), 3, 4, 143

Durang, Joeann Arter (mother), 3

Durang, Juliet (daughter), xix, 109

Durang, Mary McEwen (wife), xvii, 27, 28

"Durang's Hornpipe," 22

"The Dutch Fisherman," 44, 93

"Dwarf Dance," 23, 24

Easterly, George (Philadelphia), 33, 149

Eckert, Peter (Hanover), 121, 128, 129, 132

Emberton, Mr., 109

Entwistle, James, 109, 162

Entwistle, Mrs., 109, 162

Evans, Mr. (treasurer), 111, 112

Evans, Charles (Reading), 113

Eveland, Mr. (Quebec), 86

Fairhaven, Vt., 54

Farmer, Pennsylvania, his characteristics, 5–6

Fauster, Mrs., 139

Fechtig, Christian (Hagerstown), 129, 130

Fennel, James, 107, 156

File, *see* Phile

Finley, Mr. (Baltimore), 139, 140

Fitzpatrick (captain of bandits), 10

Floar, Mr. (machinist), 36, 108, 150

Forbisher, Mr., 79

Forrest, Edwin, xiii

Fort Ann, N.Y., *see* Whitehall

Fortune, Mrs. (New York), 22, 147

The Forty Thieves, 131

Foster, Mrs., 137

Fox, Gilbert, 109, 153

Francis, William, 107, 110, 127, 155

Francis, Mrs., 108, 158

Franklin, Benjamin, xii, xiv, 9

Franklin, Thomas, 45, 46, 97, 151

Fredericktown, Md., 127, 128, 129, 130, 138–139

French army, 7

Frobisher, Joseph, 152

Fulenton, Mr., 108, 159

Galbreath, Mr., 109

Gamblers, 6

Gay, Mr., 20, 146

Georgetown, Va., 100, 101

Gerard, Monsieur (French ambassador), 7, 8

German, Durang acts in, 115

Gettysburg, Pa., 132

The Ghost, 79

Gibbons, Mr. (tailor), 108

Gillasbie, Miss, 109

Gillasbie, Mrs., 109

Gillingham, Mr. (musician), 108, 157

Gillingham, Mrs., 108, 158

Gillis, Mr. (Montreal), 68

Gisler, Mrs. (Baltimore), 28, 29, 97

Goodwin, Mr., 109, 119

Governer (horse), 47, 54

Gray, Mrs. (wardrobe mistress), 112

Green, Mr. (Plattsburgh), 60

Green, Mr., 107, 109, 156, 161

Griffin, Mr. (Whitehall), 52

Gross, Mr., 107, 156

Guaran, Mr., 35

Guardie, Madame, 36, 150

Hagerstown, Md., 128, 129, 130, 138
Hallam, Lewis, life, xi, 144, 153; as actor, 16, 19, 29, 31; as producer, xii, 12, 18, 26, 30
Hallam, Mrs. (Miss Tuke), 20
Hamilton, Mr., 42, 150
Hammilton, Andrew (Philadelphia), 9
Hanes, Mr. (Philadelphia coachmaker), 118
Hanover, Pa., Durang in, 120, 121, 127, 128, 129, 130, 132
Harbaugh, Mr. (tailor), 12
Harding, Mr., 108, 157
Harding, Mrs., 108, 158
Harlequen Touchstone, 19
Harmony Hall (Philadelphia), 110, 127, 132
Harper, Joseph, 20, 23
Harper, Mrs., 20, 147
Harponga (Quebec), 92
Harris, Joseph, 109, 132, 160
Harrisburg, Pa., Durang there, xii, 113, 114, 119, 120, 131, 132, 134; court in, 119–121; July 4th celebration, 134–135
Harwood, John, 109, 153, 163
Harrowgate Garden (Philadelphia), 33
Hartford, Conn., 38
Hathwell, Mr., 109, 160
Heard, Mr., 20, 146
Henry, Joseph, as actor, 19, 31; as producer, 19, 21, 35, 38, 145
Henry, Mrs. (Maria Storer), 20, 21, 147
Herbert, Mr., 109
"The High Mettled Racer," 92

Hodgkinson, John, 35, 36, 38, 149
Hodgkinson, Mrs., 36, 149
Hoffmaster, Mr. (New York), 22
Holland, John Joseph, 108, 112, 157
Holliday Street Theatre (Baltimore), xviii
Hopkins, Mr., 109, 161
Horsemanship, Durang learns, 43, 69, 118
Horton, Mr., 109, 134
Horton, Mrs., 134, 135
Howard's Park (Baltimore), 121
Howe, General William, 6
Hudson, N.Y., 48
Hughes, Mr., 104, 109
Hughsten, Mr. (Fredericktown), 139
Humrick, Mr. (Carlisle), 128, 129
Hupfield, Mr. (musician), 118
Hutchins, Master, 43, 45, 47, 68, 95, 103
Hutchins, Mr. (groom), 46, 57, 88, 90
Hyde, Miss, 12
Hyneman, Frederick (Harrisburg), 132, 133, 134

Indians, 63, 64, 70–74
Irvin, Mr. (Hagerstown), 138
Isle of Orleans (Quebec), 89

Jackson, Mr., 109
Jackson, Mrs., 109
Jacobs, Mr., 109, 160
Jacobs, Mrs., 109, 132, 162
Jefferie, Mrs., 129
Jefferson, Mrs. Joseph, 109, 162
Jefferson, Thomas, 109, 160

John Street Theatre (New York), 22, 38
Johnson, Mr., 35, 109, 149, 161
Jonas, Mr. (Montreal), 75
Jones, Mr., 109, 130, 160
Jones, Mrs., 109, 162

Kean, Edmund, 141–142, 153
Kenna Family, 27, 34, 147–148
Kenney, Mr. (singer), 149
Kernan, John (Carlisle), 135
Kimble, Mrs. (Fredericktown), 139
King, William, 36, 39, 109, 137, 139, 149
Kinney, Mr., 35
Kinsler, John (Montreal), 74, 75, 76
Kinsler, Widow (Montreal), 74
Klipstine, Mr., 28
Kniphousen, General, 6

Lachine, Quebec, 70, 73
Lady Washington (horse), 47
Lafayette Theatre (New York), xix
La Feever, Mr. (Laprairie), 66
Lailson's Circus, 101, 102, 105
Lake, Mr., 20, 146
Lake Champlain, 53, 57, 60, 61, 62, 90, 91
Lancaster, Pa., xii, 3, 4, 6, 7, 10, 46, 96, 111, 113, 114, 119, 127, 128, 129, 132
L'Ancienne Lorette, Quebec, 87, 89
Lansingburgh, N.Y., 92
Laprairie, Quebec, 66, 67, 90
La Tortue, Quebec, 64
Leahman, Thomas (Baltimore), 118, 127
Lebanon, Pa., 14

Lecture upon Heads, 16, 144
Leg, Mr., 109
Leg, Mrs., 109
L'Estrange, Mr., 107, 156
L'Estrange, Miss, 108
Lewis, Mr., 109
Liberty Hall (Vermont), 55
Little Boner (horse), 47
Little Devil, *see* Redigé, Paolo
Loaft, Mr., 109, 119
Lopez, Don, 109, 161
Lucas, Mr., 109
Lulier, Mr., 44

Marriott, Mr., 41, 150
Marriott, Mrs., 150
Marshall, Mr., 107, 156
Marshall, Mrs., 108, 159
Martin, John, 29, 109, 160
Maskinonge, Quebec, 82, 88,
McCubbin, Mr. (tailor), 112
McFarland, Mr., 109, 160
McFarland, Mrs., 109
McGinnis, James, 40–41
McIntosh, Colonel (Montreal), 79
McKenney, Mr., 109
McKenzie, Mr., 42, 108, 159
McKeon, Thomas (Governor of Pennsylvania), 96, 152
McTavish, Simon (fur trader), 79, 151–152
Melmouth, Mrs., 109, 161
Mennonites, 114–115
Merry, Ann, 108, 157
Mestayer, Louis, 109, 118, 161
Mestayer, Mrs., 109, 162
Milbourn, Charles, 108, 157
Milbourne, Miss, 108, 158
Miller, John D., 42, 109, 161

Miller, Mr. (carpenter), 103
Miller, Jacob (Fredericktown), 129
Mountmorency, Quebec, 80, 90
Montcalm, General Louis Joseph de, 89
Montgomery, General Richard, 89, 90
Montreal, Quebec, 67, 73, 80, 88, 89
Moore, Judge (Chazy), 62
Moore, Mr., 16
Moore, Mrs. (Chazy), 62
Moreton, John Pollard, 107, 155
Morgan, Mr., 109, 130
Morris, Owen, 20, 109, 146, 161
Morris, Mrs., 109, 147, 162
Morris, Robert (Philadelphia), 37, 46
Mullen, Miss, 109, 118, 119, 121, 129
"Mother Brown's Retreat," 28

New York (city), 22, 23, 24, 30, 31, 41, 42, 45, 93
Noise's Inn (Whitehall), 53
Norristown, Pa., 116
North American Bank (Philadelphia), 132
Northern Liberty Company, Durang forms, 34; members, 35
Nugent, Mr., 41

Old American Company, Durang joins, 36; first American performance of, 153–154; members, 19–20, 36, 145–147; mentioned, 28, 31, 38, 40
Oldmixon, Sir John, 109, 162
Oldmixon, Mrs., 108, 158
Olympic Theatre (Philadelphia), 141

Les Ombres Chinoise, 19, 26
Pantheon (Baltimore), 121, 127
Park Theatre (New York), xix
Parks, Baltimore, *see* Columbia Garden, Howard's Park, Pavilion Garden; Philadelphia, *see* Harrowgate Garden, Vauxhall Gardens
Patterson, Mr., 42, 150
Pavilion Garden (Baltimore), 139–140
Peale, Charles Willson (artist), xii, 19, 145
Pellisiere, M. (composer), 36, 37, 150
Pennsylvania Dutch Circuit, xv–xvi; Durang begins, 113; principles, 115, 116, 122; members of company, 119, 121, 129, 130, 132, 133, 134, 137; plays, xiii, 122–126
Perry's Victory, 133
Petersburg, Pa., 132
Pettit, Miss, 109
Phile, Mr., 20, 22
Philadelphia, Pa., xii, xiii, xvi, xix, 7, 9, 10, 21, 24, 29, 32, 46, 69, 89, 101, 106–107, 113, 114, 120, 127, 132, 141
Placide, Alexander, 30, 31, 32, 148
Placide, Madame, 32, 109, 148
Platt, Esq. (Plattsburgh), 60
Plattsburgh, N.Y., 59, 60, 90
Pointe aux Trembles, Quebec, 81
Pomroy, Captain (La Tortue), 64, 65, 66
Pomroy, Mrs. (La Tortue), 65
The Poor Soldier, 22, 26
Powell, Charles S., 150
Pownall, Mrs., 36, 149–150

Prescott, General Robert (Governor of Quebec), 86–87
Prigmore, Mr., 36, 109, 150
Prigmore, Miss, 109
Puppet theatre, Durang's, 25, 26
Pursell, Mr., 35, 149

Quebec (city), 85, 86, 87, 89
Quenet (dancer), 36, 37, 150

Rankin, Mr. & Mrs., 42, 150
Reading, Pa., 116, 119
Recollêt Gate (Montreal), 67, 76
Redigé, Paolo (Little Devil), 30, 148
Regiment de Waldner, 3
Reinagle, Alexander, 37, 106, 107, 112
Revolutionary War, 6
Rhode Island, 38
Rice's Inn (Fairhaven), 54
Ricketts, Francis, 43, 44, 45, 46, 80, 95, 103, 104, 151
Ricketts, John Bill, 35, 42–103 *passim;* 106, 110
Ricketts' Circus, members, 43, 47, 94; tour of South, 98–101; tour of Canada, 46–93; burns down, 96
Rickey, Samuel (Philadelphia), 113, 114
"Riding the Tailor" (equestrian act), 77
Rivière du Loup, Quebec, 82, 88
Roach, Mr., 118
Robbins, Luke (painter), 36, 100, 108, 112, 149, 159
Robinson Crusoe, 70
Robinson, J., 20, 28, 109, 146, 161
Rogers, Mrs. (Basin Harbor), 56, 57

Rohrer, M. (Lancaster), 113, 119, 127, 128, 129
Romeo and Juliet, 142
Rouse, Mr. (Skeensborough), 90
Rouses Point, N.Y., 61
Rowson, Mr., 44, 95, 96
Rowson, Mrs., 44, 95
Rusell, Mr., 11, 29
Rutherford, Mr., 109, 163
Ryan, Dennis, 144
Ryan, Mr. (prompter), 20, 28, 146

St. Charles River (Quebec), 89
St. Johns, Quebec, 61, 66, 67, 90, 91
St. John's Gate (Quebec), 86
St. Lawrence River, 67, 70, 74, 76, 81, 88, 89, 90
St. Mary River (Quebec), 84
Sandy Hill, N.Y., 51
San Sulpice, Quebec, 81
Sanders, Mr., 109
Savage, Mr., 109, 137, 139
Savage, Mrs., 109, 137, 139
Savelle, Mrs. (housekeeper), 112
Scrivener, Thomas, 109, 160
Seerson, Mr., 109
Seymour, Joseph, 42, 109, 129, 150, 161
Seymour, Mrs., 42, 109, 129, 150
Seymour, Miss, 161
Shakespear's Jubilee, 23
Sharnock, Charles, 109, 161
Shaw, Mrs., 108, 158
Shenegrave, Mr., (Quebec C.), 86
Sheneman, Mr., 133
She Stoops to Conquer, xvi
Shippensburg, Pa., 131, 136
Shitz, Mr. (informer), 21

Shyock, Mr. (Chambersburg), 136

The Siege of Qxetrace [Gaza], 44

Silver Heels (horse), 47

Simpson, Mrs., 109, 162

Skeensborough, N.Y., 53, 90, 91

Smith, Mr. (Hagerstown), 128

Snider, Mr. (Harrisburg), 114

Snyder, Jacob (painter), 20, 24, 28, 147

Snyder, John (Chambersburg), 128, 129, 130, 137

Solomon, Miss, 109

Solomon, Mrs., 161

Southwark Theatre (Philadelphia), 8, 11, 12, 16, 26, 36, 92, 96, 127, 142, 144, 152

Spayd, John (Reading), 116

Spinacuta, Signor, 43, 44

Spinacuta, Signora, 43, 151

Stallings, Mr. (Fredericktown), 127, 128

Steover, Esquire (Lebanon), 114

Stewart, Mr., 149

Stoffle Rilbps or *The Seu Shwain Wedding*, xvi

Stony Point, N.Y., 47

The Stranger (Kotzebue), xvi

Strickland, Mr. (carpenter), 108, 112, 159

Stuard, Mrs., 35

Sully, Mat (clown), 43, 44, 103, 150

Suverre River (Quebec), 84

Taylor, Mr., 109

Templeman, William, 11, 100, 144

Theatrical companies, *see* Chestnut Street Theatre, Northern Liberty Co., Old American Co., Pennsylvania Dutch Circuit, Wall and Ryan Co., Wignell and Reinagle Co.

Theatres, Baltimore, *see* Holliday Street Theatre, Pantheon; New York, *see* John Street Theatre, Lafayette Theatre, Park Theatre; Philadelphia, *see* Chestnut Street Theatre, Olympic Theatre, Southwark Theatre

Thompson, Mr., 109

Thornton, Mr., 121

Threatwell, Mr. (St. Johns), 61

Tobine, Mr., 35

Tom Thumb (Fielding), xix

Tomkins, Mr. and Mrs., 44

Tomlinson, Mr., Jr., 46

Tommoa, Captain, 70, 71–72

Tracy, Mr., 32

Trois Rivières, Quebec, 83, 84

Troy, N.Y., 92

Tuke, Miss, 147

Turney, Thomas, 109

Turnner, Mr., 14

Twaits, Mr., 108, 159

Umrich, Mr. (Carlisle), 120

Usher, Mr., 109, 160

Val, M., 36, 150

Val, Madame, 36

Varennes, Quebec, 76

Vaughan, Mr., 35, 149

Vauxhall Gardens (Philadelphia), 33–34, 35, 141, 149

Vermont, 53, 55

Vestres (dancer), 18

Wall, Thomas, 144

Wall and Ryan Company, 11, 12, 42, 144

Wallace, James, xix, 109, 160
Wallach, Mrs., 109
War of 1812, 133
Ward, Mr., 112
Waring, Leigh, 109, 161
Waring, Mrs., 109, 162
Warrel, A., Sr., 107, 155
Warrell, James, 107, 156
Warrell, Mrs., 108, 158
Warrell, Thomas, 107, 156
Warren, William, 107, 112, 118, 141, 155
Warren, Mrs., 108, 153, 158
Washington, George, 7, 27, 42, 46
Washington, D.C., 113, 119
"Washington's March," 48
Webster, Benjamin, 109, 163
Weedley, Mr., 109
Wells, Mr. (treasurer—Chestnut St. Theatre), 111
Wells, Miss, 35, 149
Wentz's Hotel (Lancaster), 132
West, James, 36, 37, 149
West, Samuel, 36
Weston, Mr., 20, 146
West Point, N.Y., 48
Whitehall, N.Y., 53, 91
White, Miss, 109, 133, 162
Whiteside, Mr. (Lancaster), 129
Whitlock, Charles, 107, 155
Whitlock, Mrs., 108, 157–158

Willes, Mr., 109
Willet, Captain, 47, 49
Willing, Thomas, 37
Wilmot, Mr., 109, 161
Wilt, Peter (York), 129, 132, 133
Wignell, Thomas, 20, 27, 37, 105, 106, 107, 110, 117, 145–146
Wignell, Mrs., 117
Wignell and Reinagle Company, 37, 105, 107–109
Wolfe, General James, 89–90
Wolf, Mr., 28
Wood, Mr. (treasurer), 108, 111
Wood, Mrs. (Reading), 116, 119
Wood, William, xiii, 141
Woodham, Mr., 109, 163
Woodham, Mrs., 109, 163
Wools, Stephen, 20, 58, 145
Wooster, General David, 89
Wright, Isaac (L. Champlain), 58
Wyeth, John (Harrisburg), 131, 153

Yamachiche, Quebec, 83
York, Pa., xix, 4, 5, 6, 7, 46, 127, 129, 132, 133

Ziegler's Hotel (Harrisburg), 131